YORK NOTES

RICHARD III

WILLIAM SHAKESPEARE

NOTES BY TREVOR MILLUM

 Longman

Exterior picture of the Globe Theatre reproduced by permission of the Raymond Mander and Joe Mitchenson Theatre Collection

The right of Trevor Millum to be identified as Author of this Work
has been asserted by him in accordance with the Copyright,
Designs and Patents Act 1988

YORK PRESS
322 Old Brompton Road, London SW5 9JH

PEARSON EDUCATION LIMITED
Edinburgh Gate, Harlow,
Essex CM20 2JE, United Kingdom
Associated companies, branches and representatives throughout the world

First published 2007
Second impression 2007

ISBN: 978–1–4058–5646–1

Illustrated by Bob Farley; and Neil Gower (p. 6 only)
Phototypeset by utimestwo, Northamptonshire
Printed in Great Britain by Henry Ling Limited, at the Dorset Press, Dorchester, DT1 1HD.

The author of these Notes is Trevor Millum, an experienced writer and editor of study guides. He is also a former Head of English

CONTENTS

These York Notes aim to help you get the very best result in your Key Stage 3 test on *Richard III*, but also enable you to enjoy your study, too. They will help you approach the test with confidence knowing that you have been given guidance on the **four key areas** you will be tested on:

- the characters and their motivation

- important ideas, themes and issues that run through the play

- the use of language in the text and its effects

- your understanding of how the play might be performed or staged

THE TEST ITSELF

In the test you will be expected to answer a question on **two extracts** from *Richard III*. The question will ask you about one of the four key areas above, for example:

Act I Scene 2 lines 115–230

Act III Scene 4 lines 1–78

What impression do you get of Richard in these two extracts?

You will have **45 minutes** to write on the extracts from *Richard III*.

HOW THESE YORK NOTES WILL HELP

These Notes are divided up into sections which will help you answer questions such as the one above. You will find some background on Shakespeare – what do we know about him? What was it like going to the theatre in his day? Then, clear summaries of **every scene** will guide you through the play. In Part Three you'll find individual sections on the four key areas. Finally, these Notes will also help you with the test itself. You will be given guidance on exam technique, how to structure your answer, how to improve your level, and so on.

In the end, these Notes are designed to help you enjoy the play as you study it. They are not a substitute for reading the play but should help you make sense of Shakespeare's ideas and language, and gain a clear picture of how the characters behave, and why they act as they do.

The text used in these Notes is the Longman School Shakespeare edition, 2004.

PART ONE

INTRODUCTION

HOW TO STUDY A SHAKESPEARE PLAY

It may seem obvious, but it is important to remember that you are studying a play, a text that is meant to be performed. You should keep in mind that the words you see on the page are brought to life when they are acted out.

It is also important you keep in mind the **four key areas** you will be tested on. But what exactly do they mean?

1. **CHARACTER** and **MOTIVATION**: this means what a character is *like* (ambitious? innocent? evil?), what they *do* (kill someone? fall in love? wear a disguise?) and *why* they behave in this way (is their motive to get revenge because they have been betrayed? or perhaps because they feel jealous?).

2. **IDEAS, THEMES** and **ISSUES** in the play: this means the things that interested Shakespeare and he wanted the audience to think about. For example, what happens if someone desires something they can't have? Or, what problems do people have ruling a kingdom? It could also be the wider ideas that are explored in a play: different types of ambition, love, family conflict, death, and so on.

3. The way Shakespeare uses **LANGUAGE** in the text: this means the different ways ideas in the play are expressed. For example, the use of powerful words or phrases to show how people feel, e.g. Margaret: 'Thou elvish-marked, abortive, rooting hog!'; or the use of unusual images, e.g. Hastings: 'More pity that the eagles should be mewed / Whiles kites and buzzards prey at liberty.'

4. How the text works in **PERFORMANCE**: this means thinking about different ways the play might be staged and performed. For example, how do Clarence's murderers show their emotions? How can battles be presented on stage? How can Richard's character be shown in the way he speaks, moves, or even how he dresses?

EXAMINER'S SECRET

Always keep in mind that *Richard III* is a play. It was never meant to be read like a book, so try to imagine scenes such as the battle in Act V being performed on a stage in front of a live audience.

GLOSSARY

elvish-marked marked at birth by evil fairies

mewed caged

Born **1564**

Marries Anne Hathaway **1582**

First plays performed and poems published **1590 onwards**

Richard III written **1593**

Joins acting company **1594**

Buys New Place, a large house in Stratford **1597**

Moves to the Globe Theatre **1599**

Takes over Blackfriars Theatre **1608**

Globe Theatre burns down **1613**

Dies and is buried in Stratford **1616**

WHO WAS SHAKESPEARE?

We actually know very little for certain about Shakespeare as no
personal records survive, such as diaries, letters and so on. What we
do have are references to him from other people, one of the earliest
being an insult: Shakespeare was called an 'upstart crow' – which
suggests the writer may have been rather jealous of his success! We
do know that Shakespeare came from quite a wealthy background
– his father was a successful merchant – and we also know that he
married young: at eighteen, to an older woman, Anne, who was
twenty-six. We know, too, that his son Hamnet died at the relatively
young age of eleven, and while it was common for children to die at
a young age during this period, we can imagine the sorrow this
event must have caused. Many of Shakespeare's plays explore
relationships between fathers and sons, and of course the name of
the hero in his most famous play, *Hamlet*, is remarkably close in
spelling to that of his own son.

It is likely, too, that he spent many years away from Anne in
London, and while we don't know enough about their relationship
to say accurately whether the marriage was a happy one or not, we
can imagine that London would have seemed an attractive place to
him. It was a time of a great outburst in writing, art and music
(often referred to as the Renaissance) and Shakespeare would
probably have been excited by the range of new ideas and
possibilities available to playwrights at this time.

Most importantly, though, we need to understand that Shakespeare
was a working writer and actor, a skilled craftsman who was also a
clever businessman. He earned a living from his plays, which were
popular both with the rulers of the day (Elizabeth I and then
James I) and the ordinary public. His progress from budding writer
and actor to owner and manager of theatres, and the fact that he was
eventually able to buy the second largest house in his hometown of
Stratford, demonstrates how successful he was.

Finally, it is worth noting that Shakespeare was not just an actor and
playwright. He also wrote poetry and his Sonnets are almost as

DID YOU KNOW?
Renaissance is a
word that comes
from French and
means 'rebirth'. It is
used to describe a
very creative time
from the mid
fifteenth century to
the mid sixteenth
century, when
writers, artists and
musicians appeared
with new and
exciting ideas.

famous as his plays. What is most intriguing about them is that they seem to be addressed to two particular people. Many are addressed to a 'dark lady', while others are written to a young man, possibly a nobleman or lord. Like so many other things in Shakespeare's life, we do not know definitely *who* these people were, but the poems do give us a sense of Shakespeare being a very real person, writing about real relationships (falling in love, being rejected, getting angry, and so on), and not just someone from the past whom you are made to study by your teachers!

GOING TO THE THEATRE IN SHAKESPEARE'S DAY

In Shakespeare's day, the theatre sometimes came to you! There were groups of travelling players who moved from town to town, and it is easy to forget that until the early to mid 1500s the idea of a theatre as a permanent public building was still relatively new. So you can imagine how exciting a trip to one of these new theatres was!

DID YOU KNOW?

The original Globe Theatre in London was probably built in 1599, but was not strictly 'new' as it mostly consisted of timber from an old theatre in Blackfriars. This had to be carried across London to the south bank of the Thames!

Once at the theatre, you could choose to pay for cheap tickets standing at the front as a 'groundling'. If you had more money you could pay for seats in the surrounding galleries. Wherever you were, sitting or standing, watching a Shakespeare play at the Globe, for example, would have been quite an experience! You might well have seen live animals, and heard sound effects such as thunder and a whole variety of music from drums and trumpets to whole orchestras! Plays such as *Richard III* and other histories often contained scenes of violence, bloodshed and battles, and the whole affair would have been noisy and visually stunning. As plays and theatres became more advanced, greater and greater use was made of trapdoors, and other ways of creating special effects, but the scenery itself remained quite basic for some years. Costumes, on the other hand, were generally magnificent. It may seem strange that there are sudden dances, songs or magical appearances in some of Shakespeare's plays (sometimes with little connection to the plot!), but it is likely audiences would not have minded as they had come to the theatre for much more than just a good story. In any case, they must have enjoyed themselves, for as many as 3,000 people often stood or sat for several hours to watch a performance, regardless of the weather!

In contrast, going to the theatre today is a more formal experience, although open-air theatres, such as the rebuilt Globe and the Regent's Park theatre, do still exist. We have also kept the idea of different prices of tickets, although it is very rare to stand to watch a performance nowadays. Scenery and staging are now very sophisticated in comparison.

The key point from all this is that Shakespeare's plays were written to be performed. His plays were designed as whole entertainment packages with opportunities to laugh, cry or gasp in shock or surprise. Keeping this in mind as you study or reflect on the play is quite useful, whether you are looking at **characters**, **themes**, **language** or **performance**.

DID YOU KNOW?

In spite of the small stage, Shakespeare wrote lots of scenes with crowds, and at certain times the actors would probably have spilled over into the audience. Some of the wealthier spectators would have sat on the stage, blurring the distinction between actors and audience even more.

THE GLOBE THEATRE,

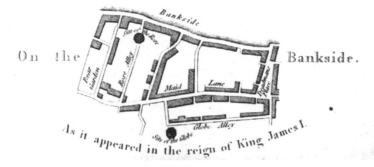

On the Bankside.

As it appeared in the reign of King James I.

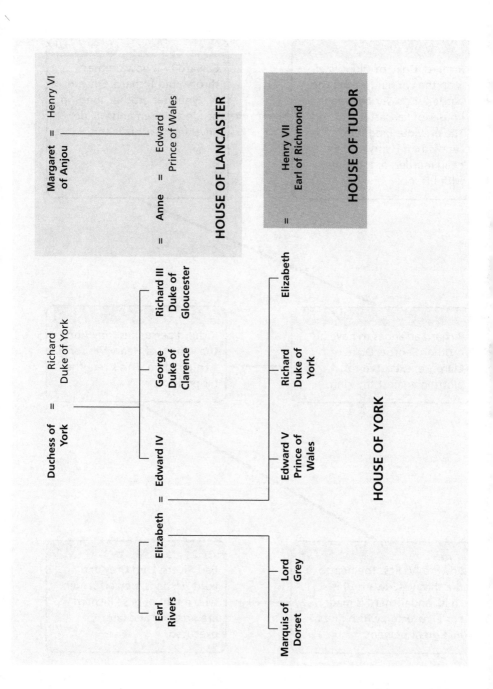

HOUSE OF LANCASTER

Margaret = Henry VI
of Anjou

Anne = Edward
Prince of Wales

HOUSE OF TUDOR

= Henry VII
Earl of Richmond

HOUSE OF YORK

Duchess of = Richard
York Duke of York

Edward IV

George
Duke of
Clarence

Richard III
Duke of
Gloucester

Elizabeth = Edward IV

Earl
Rivers

Elizabeth

Lord
Grey

Marquis of
Dorset

Edward V
Prince of
Wales

Richard
Duke of
York

Elizabeth

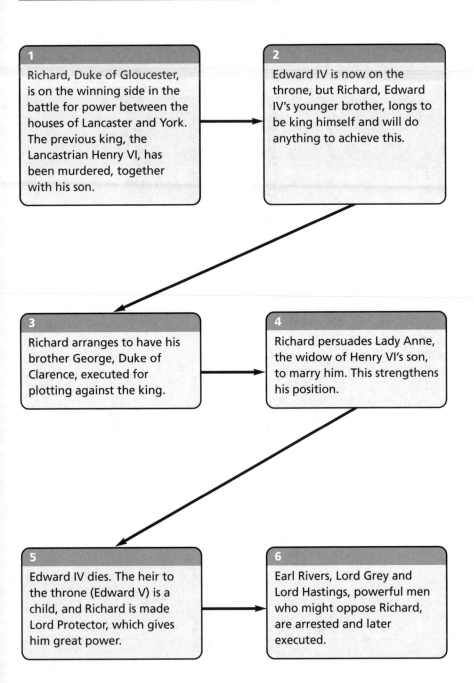

1
Richard, Duke of Gloucester, is on the winning side in the battle for power between the houses of Lancaster and York. The previous king, the Lancastrian Henry VI, has been murdered, together with his son.

2
Edward IV is now on the throne, but Richard, Edward IV's younger brother, longs to be king himself and will do anything to achieve this.

3
Richard arranges to have his brother George, Duke of Clarence, executed for plotting against the king.

4
Richard persuades Lady Anne, the widow of Henry VI's son, to marry him. This strengthens his position.

5
Edward IV dies. The heir to the throne (Edward V) is a child, and Richard is made Lord Protector, which gives him great power.

6
Earl Rivers, Lord Grey and Lord Hastings, powerful men who might oppose Richard, are arrested and later executed.

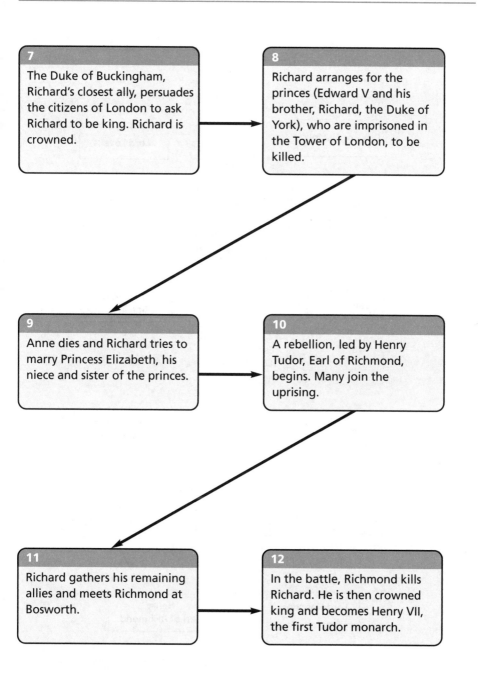

7
The Duke of Buckingham, Richard's closest ally, persuades the citizens of London to ask Richard to be king. Richard is crowned.

8
Richard arranges for the princes (Edward V and his brother, Richard, the Duke of York), who are imprisoned in the Tower of London, to be killed.

9
Anne dies and Richard tries to marry Princess Elizabeth, his niece and sister of the princes.

10
A rebellion, led by Henry Tudor, Earl of Richmond, begins. Many join the uprising.

11
Richard gathers his remaining allies and meets Richmond at Bosworth.

12
In the battle, Richmond kills Richard. He is then crowned king and becomes Henry VII, the first Tudor monarch.

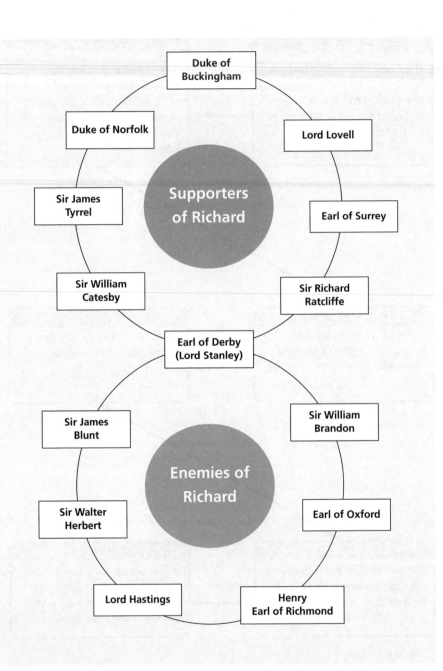

Duke of
Buckingham

Duke of Norfolk

Lord Lovell

Sir James
Tyrrel

**Supporters
of Richard**

Earl of Surrey

Sir William
Catesby

Sir Richard
Ratcliffe

Earl of Derby
(Lord Stanley)

Sir James
Blunt

Sir William
Brandon

**Enemies of
Richard**

Sir Walter
Herbert

Earl of Oxford

Lord Hastings

Henry
Earl of Richmond

PART TWO

SUMMARIES

ACT I

SCENE 1 – RICHARD PLOTS TO SEIZE POWER

1. **Richard shares his plans with the audience.**
2. **He blames his physical deformities for making him a villain.**
3. **His brother Clarence is taken to the Tower of London.**

When the play starts, Richard, Duke of Gloucester, speaks directly to the audience. The bad times of war – 'the winter of our discontent' – are over because the king, his eldest brother, 'this son of York', has triumphed (lines 1–2). However, peacetime does not suit Richard. He was born with several physical deformities – he is 'Deformed, unfinished' (line 20) – which he blames for his character. He reveals his evil intentions to us and seems proud of his villainy.

From the very beginning, Richard is plotting to seize power. His first target is his brother George, Duke of Clarence. If Edward IV dies, Clarence (as Richard's older brother) would have a stronger claim to the throne than Richard. So Richard has spread a rumour 'By drunken prophecies, libels, and dreams' (line 33) that someone whose name begins with G will murder the king's sons.

Clarence enters, guarded by Sir Robert Brakenbury, the lieutenant of the Tower of London, and his soldiers. Richard tells his brother that his imprisonment is all the fault of King Edward's wife, Queen Elizabeth ('Lady Grey'), and her relations ('kindred') and the king's mistress, Lady Shore. Richard promises Clarence that he will do what he can to help him. As soon as Clarence is out of sight, however, he reveals to the audience that he has no intention of coming to his brother's assistance, except to help him on his way to heaven!

CHECKPOINT 1

What is the effect of having Richard speak directly to you?

 DID YOU KNOW?

Richard is making a **pun** when he talks about 'this son of York' (son/sun). Edward IV's father was Richard, Duke of York, who was killed in battle in 1460. But the sun was also an emblem of the king, and Edward IV's badge in particular.

GLOSSARY

libels lies about someone

Lord Hastings, the Lord Chamberlain, now appears. Recently released from the Tower of London, he is determined to get his own back on those who caused his imprisonment. Once Hastings is out of the way, Richard can yet again speak honestly to the audience. He hopes the king will die, but not 'Till George be packed with posthorse up to heaven' (line 146) – in other words, not until Clarence is sent to his death swiftly.

The final part of Richard's plot is to marry Lady Anne Neville, the Earl of Warwick's daughter and the widow of Henry VI's son – whom Richard killed in battle. This marriage to one of the most important noblewomen in the country would help to secure his grip on power.

A villain with two faces

This first scene sets up the action for the rest of the play. In it, Richard reveals his character and his plans to the audience but hides them from those he meets. When he is on his own on stage he tells us that he is 'determinèd to prove a villain' (line 30). We can believe what he says to *us* – but not a word of what he says to others!

The actor playing Richard must use all his skill in order to involve the audience in what he is planning. Even if we don't feel sympathy for him, we must at least be interested in *what* he is attempting and *how* he might achieve it. His first speech is famous and reveals Richard's skill with words.

? DID YOU KNOW?

Shakespeare was not concerned with historical accuracy. He wrote *Richard III* in the reign of Elizabeth I, a direct descendant of Henry VII, and was keen to show the Tudors in a good light.

What happened before?

Shakespeare's audience would have known about the events which happened before the play starts. A modern audience probably does not! The king, Edward IV, has recently regained the throne after a long civil war between two powerful families – the Yorkists and the Lancastrians. Henry VI, the last of the kings of the house of Lancaster, has been defeated. He and his son (another Edward) have been killed in battle by the Duke of Gloucester.

The Yorkist king Edward IV is now on the throne. He has two younger brothers: George, Duke of Clarence; and Richard, Duke of Gloucester.

SCENE 2 – ANNE MOURNS AND RICHARD WOOS HER

1 **Lady Anne mourns her husband and father-in-law's deaths.**

2 **She curses Richard.**

3 **Richard tries to convince Anne of his love for her.**

Lady Anne, the widow of Edward, Henry VI's son, enters with the corpse of her father-in-law, Henry VI. She mourns the deaths of her husband and father-in-law and curses Richard for being the cause of their deaths.

When Richard enters she repeats her curses to his face. Richard says that his love for her was a motive for killing her husband, Edward; and he tells her that he wants to marry her. Finally he persuades her to take his ring.

CHECKPOINT 2

How might the actors playing Richard and Anne make this scene believable? What reasons could she have for giving in?

GLOSSARY

packed with posthorse sent as quickly as possible, by express

When Anne leaves the stage, Richard shares with the audience his astonishment. He admits that he's not worth half of 'that brave prince' Edward (line 240) and reveals that he 'will not keep her long' (line 230).

> ### A dramatic moment
>
> As part of his attempt to persuade Anne, Richard places his sword in her hands. He bares his chest and invites her to kill him. She cannot do it. He offers to kill himself if she will order him to do so. Again, she does not. Perhaps she half believes his words, because a little later she says how pleased she is 'To see you are become so penitent' (line 221).

SCENE 3 – RICHARD SETS HIS PLOTS IN MOTION

1 **Queen Elizabeth worries what will happen if her husband dies.**

2 **Queen Margaret curses Richard and warns that he is evil.**

3 **Richard hires murderers to kill Clarence.**

Queen Elizabeth, the wife of Edward IV, is worried what will happen to her and her young children if Edward dies. Richard accuses her and her relations (Earl Rivers, Lord Grey and the Marquis of Dorset) of plotting against his brother Clarence. Margaret, widow of King Henry VI and the former queen of England, curses Richard for killing her husband and son and stealing her kingdom. She warns all of them to beware of Richard. She tells the Duke of Buckingham to 'take heed of yonder dog!' (line 288), but he ignores her.

Richard again confides in the audience how 'I clothe my naked villainy' (line 335). He meets the two men he has hired to murder Clarence, using the official papers he has obtained.

CHECKPOINT 3

Historically, Margaret actually died before Edward IV died. Why do you think Shakespeare made her a major character in the play?

Curses

Cursing – both saying bad things to someone and wishing them bad luck – is a major feature in the play. No one is better at it than Margaret. She curses almost everyone for promises they have broken and their responsibility in the killing of her husband and son. She cries: 'you were standers by ... when my son / Was stabbed with bloody daggers' (lines 209–11). She reserves her strongest curses for Richard, murderer of her husband and son, calling him an 'abortive, rooting hog!', a 'bottled spider' and 'a bunch-backed toad!' (lines 227, 241 and 245), for example.

CHECKPOINT 4

How many people does Margaret curse? Make a list and tick the names off each time one of them is killed.

Prophecy

Margaret is also full of prophecies – predictions about the future. She predicts a bad end for all of her enemies, and as the play progresses we see her words come true. When Buckingham ignores her warning about Richard, she calls herself 'a prophetess' (line 300).

 DID YOU KNOW?

Clarence's murderers have more lines to speak in the play than both the young princes put together.

SCENE 4 – THE MURDER OF CLARENCE

1 **Clarence describes his dream.**

2 **The murderers enter and kill him.**

George, Duke of Clarence, imprisoned in the Tower of London, describes his vivid dream in which he drowns after being accidentally pushed overboard by Richard. The hired murderers enter, show their official papers to Sir Robert Brakenbury, the lieutenant of the Tower, and are allowed to go to Clarence. They discuss what they are about to do, showing signs of conscience. Clarence pleads with them to 'Relent, and save your souls' (line 244), but is stabbed by the first murderer. The second murderer does not help him.

GLOSSARY

penitent sorry for what one has done

abortive unnatural

bottled bottle-shaped, swollen

bunch-backed hunchbacked

Relent Stop and have mercy

CHECKPOINT 5

Most of *Richard III* is written in blank verse. This means lines which have a regular metre or rhythm but no rhyme. The lines vary slightly in length but are usually ten syllables long. Occasionally Shakespeare switches from blank verse and writes in prose, which is a more basic and informal type of language. Clarence's two murderers speak to each other in prose. Why do you think this is?

Dreams and nightmares

An Elizabethan audience would have been convinced that dreams had deep meanings. Clarence's 'fearful dreams' (line 3) show his anxieties and uncertainties. They also show his command of powerful, poetic language, which the audience would have enjoyed. In addition, his nightmare reminds Clarence of bad deeds he has done: 'I have done these things / That now give evidence against my soul' (lines 66–7).

Now take a break!

WHO SAYS ...?

1 'I – that am not shaped for sportive tricks'

....

2 'But dead they are, and, devilish slave, by thee!'

....

4 'Thou elvish-marked, abortive, rooting hog!'

....

3 'Would all were well! But that will never be.'

....

5 'O do not slander him, for he is kind!'

....

CHECK THE PLOT

6 What does Richard blame for his behaviour?

....

7 Why has Clarence been imprisoned?

....

9 Why is Lady Anne important to Richard?

....

8 Why might Clarence prevent Richard becoming king?

....

10 In some editions of the play, Margaret is called Queen Margaret. Why?

....

Check your answers on p. 85.

SCENE 1 – FRAGILE HARMONY IS EASILY BROKEN

① The peace of the kingdom is fragile.

② King Edward IV tries to make everyone friends.

③ He is upset to hear of his brother Clarence's death.

The king is ill; he is surrounded by nobles and courtiers. He asks them to stop fighting among themselves and 'swear your love' for one another (line 8). They promise to do so. Richard arrives and joins in the general goodwill but then reveals that Clarence is dead. The king's pardon did not reach the Tower of London in time, he says. Edward IV is upset and angry; he blames others for not trying to save Clarence. Richard blames Queen Elizabeth's relatives for Clarence's death.

DID YOU KNOW?

Richard appears in three earlier plays by Shakespeare: the three parts of *Henry VI*. He is portrayed as a nasty piece of work in those plays too!

Plotting and power

'You have been factious' says King Edward (line 20) – but this is not surprising. In the long civil war preceding the action of *Richard III*, alliances were made and broken as both sides tried to gain power. Even now, no one really trusts anyone else – and Richard can use this to his own advantage.

SCENE 2 – KING EDWARD IS DEAD

① Queen Elizabeth mourns the death of her husband, Edward IV.

② Earl Rivers recommends crowning the young Prince of Wales quickly.

③ A group goes to fetch him.

The Duchess of York, mother of Edward IV, Clarence and Richard, recognises her son Richard's 'deep vice' (line 28). Queen Elizabeth enters, saying that her husband, the king, has died. Both women express their grief loudly and at length. Elizabeth's brother,

Earl Rivers, suggests that she should find comfort in her son Edward, Prince of Wales and the heir to the throne: 'Send straight for him. / Let him be crowned' (lines 97–8). When Richard and the other courtiers enter, Buckingham also advises that Prince Edward should be brought to London to be crowned.

EXAMINER'S SECRET

Do not ignore the **stage directions**. They can tell us a lot about a **character** or the way Shakespeare intended the **audience** to see the events. The fact that Queen Elizabeth rushes in with her hair hanging loose is significant. A queen would never usually do that. This suggests her grief is real.

Royal names

The names of the kings of England at this stage in history seem to be either Edward or Henry, the only exception being Richard III. Henry VI (himself the son of the Lancastrian Henry V) had a son called Edward, who was killed (by Richard). The new Yorkist king is Edward IV, and his son, one of the 'princes in the Tower', is known as Edward V. The Earl of Richmond, who defeats Richard at the end of the play, takes the title Henry VII. His son became the famous Henry VIII!

GLOSSARY

factious plotting against one another, back-biting

vice wickedness

SCENE 3 – THE PEOPLE SMELL TROUBLE

EXAMINER'S SECRET

Seeing *Richard III* in **performance** will help you to understand and enjoy the play. If you can, try to go to a live performance on the stage, but if not there are several film versions available. The 1995 film starring Ian McKellen is very good. Remember, though, that films can make cuts and changes.

① Bystanders discuss the news.

② Rivalry at the top means more trouble for the country.

We see ordinary people in the street discussing the news of Edward IV's death. Wisely they say that there will be more trouble. They recognise that Richard is 'full of danger' (line 27) and that Queen Elizabeth's relations will cause further disharmony.

The voice of the people

Shakespeare frequently uses ordinary people to pass comments on the actions of their rulers. No one apart from the nobility had any political rights, so all they could do was watch and hope. Sometimes they might riot or rise up in rebellion, but it rarely did them any good.

In spite of this, the general support and goodwill of the population *was* important to the country's rulers. We can see that in this play when Buckingham tries to persuade the citizens of London to support Richard's claim to the crown. 'How now, how now? What say the citizens?' Richard asks Buckingham eagerly at the start of Act III Scene 7.

SCENE 4 – RICHARD BEGINS TO ASSERT HIS POWER

① Earl Rivers and Lord Grey are arrested.

② The Duchess of York, Queen Elizabeth and the young Duke of York seek a place of safety.

We see the younger of the two princes (Richard, Duke of York) with his mother, Queen Elizabeth; his grandmother, the Duchess of York; and the Archbishop of York. The other prince, heir to the throne, is on his way.

A messenger brings news that Earl Rivers and Lord Grey, the queen's brother and one of her sons by her previous marriage, have been arrested by the 'mighty Dukes' Gloucester (Richard) and Buckingham (line 45). The duchess warns that there are 'unquiet wrangling days' to come (line 56), when brother will fight brother: 'Blood to blood, self against self!' (line 64). Queen Elizabeth and the duchess, along with the young Duke of York, decide to seek sanctuary with the Church.

> ### A coup
>
> Richard is preparing to seize power in what today would be called a *coup d'état* ('coup' means hit or strike; 'état' means state or country), usually shortened to 'coup' and pronounced 'coo'. He acts swiftly, forcefully and unexpectedly against Rivers and Grey and will do so against others.

DID YOU KNOW?
Until 1623, those who were accused of crimes could seek sanctuary in a church. Here we see royalty resorting to this means of finding safety, which shows how desperate they are.

Now take a break!

GLOSSARY
unquiet restless, troubled
wrangling fighting, quarrelling

Who says ...?

1 'You have been factious one against the other.'

....

2 'Was never mother had so dear a loss.'

....

4 'O, full of danger is the Duke of Gloucester!'

....

3 'Forthwith from Ludlow the young Prince be fetched'

....

5 'Ay me, I see the ruin of my house!'

....

Check the plot

6 Why is King Edward so keen that the quarrelling nobles make peace with one another?

....

7 Why is Edward IV surprised that Clarence is dead?

....

9 Where are Earl Rivers and Lord Grey sent as prisoners?

....

8 Why does Buckingham suggest just a few people go to bring the Prince of Wales to London?

....

10 Where does Elizabeth go with her son, the young Duke of York?

....

Check your answers on p. 85.

SCENE 1 – RICHARD AND BUCKINGHAM PLAN THEIR COUP

① The princes are sent to the Tower of London.

② Richard and Buckingham plot how to seize the throne.

③ They plan to test the loyalty of Hastings.

The Prince of Wales (Edward V) has arrived. Richard and Buckingham steal his brother, the Duke of York, from the safety of the Church. Richard acts like a friendly uncle but says that his two nephews must stay, for their own protection, in the Tower of London.

Buckingham and Richard talk over their plan to have Richard crowned king. They discuss the position of two powerful men, Lord Hastings and Lord Stanley, the Earl of Derby. They agree that it will be hard to get these two on their side. Richard's solution is simple. If Hastings will not agree, then 'Chop off his head, man!' (line 193). Richard promises Buckingham that he will make him Earl of Hereford in return for his support.

> **CHECKPOINT 6**
>
> How will Buckingham and Richard find out if Hastings is on their side?

The two princes

This is the only scene where we see the young Prince Edward. It will be an important scene for the director to stage. Should the humour of the scene be stressed – or the pathos? What should Richard's manner be: jovial, reassuring, slightly threatening?

SCENE 2 – HASTINGS FAILS TO TAKE NOTICE OF THE WARNING SIGNS

① Catesby discovers Hastings will not support Richard in his aim to become king.

② Earl Rivers and Lord Grey are to be executed.

Lord Stanley, the Earl of Derby, has a vivid dream in which 'the boar had razèd off his helm' (line 11). He sends a messenger to warn Lord Hastings, the Lord Chamberlain, of danger, and advises him to flee with him 'toward the north, / To shun the danger that his soul divines' (lines 17–18). Hastings dismisses Derby's dream and his fears. Instead he says: 'the boar will use us kindly' (line 33), believing he is secure.

EXAMINER'S SECRET

When writing about this **scene** or ones immediately following it, you could refer to Richard as 'the boar'. As long as you don't overdo it, using other ways of describing **characters** adds variety to your writing and shows you know the **text**.

One of Richard's supporters, Sir William Catesby, tries to find out how Hastings would feel about Richard becoming king. Hastings makes it clear that he would not support Richard, and replies that he would 'have this crown of mine cut from my shoulders / Before I'll see the crown so foul misplaced!' (lines 43–4). Lord Stanley, Earl of Derby, brings news that Queen Elizabeth's brother and son, Earl Rivers and Lord Grey, are to be executed. But still Hastings does not fear for his own safety.

> **Appearance and reality**
>
> The play has many examples of the differences between what appears to be the case and what is really happening. We see this especially in the behaviour of Richard where he says one thing and means something different – usually the opposite. We also notice it in the character of Catesby. Pretending to be a loyal servant, he is in fact spying for Richard. He lets us know his true feelings (as Richard and Buckingham do) in asides. At the end of this scene Buckingham jokes to the audience that Hastings will be at the Tower of London longer than he thinks: he will be there not just for lunch, but 'supper too, although thou knowest it not' (line 121).

SCENE 3 – HEADS BEGIN TO ROLL

1. **Rivers and Grey are on their way to be executed.**
2. **Queen Margaret's prophecies are coming true.**

The action moves to Pomfret Castle, where Earl Rivers and Lord Grey, brother and son of Queen Elizabeth, are on their way to their execution. 'Margaret's curse is fall'n upon our heads,' says Grey (line 14). Rivers reminds the audience that she also cursed Hastings and Buckingham, 'Then cursed she Richard' (line 17).

> **CHECKPOINT 7**
>
> Do you remember when and why Queen Margaret cursed them? If not, go back and check.

SCENE 4 – HASTINGS IS ARRESTED

1. **The council of nobles, planning the coronation, is uncertain what to do.**
2. **Lord Hastings is accused of treachery and arrested.**

In the Tower of London there is a meeting of the most powerful men in the country, including the Duke of Buckingham, the Earl of Derby, Lord Hastings and the Bishop of Ely. They are supposed to be planning Edward V's coronation, but no one is quite sure how to proceed. They all fear Richard.

Richard himself enters, picks a quarrel with Hastings and sends him to be executed. Another of Margaret's curses has been fulfilled.

> **GLOSSARY**
>
> **the boar** Richard's emblem
>
> **razèd off his helm** took off his helmet, i.e. the civilised man, Richard, revealed himself to be a vicious wild animal
>
> **shun** avoid
>
> **divines** suspects, guesses
>
> **crown of mine** Hastings's head
>
> **foul** badly

Dramatic irony

Dramatic irony is the term given to a situation in a play where the audience knows more than a character on stage. When Hastings talks about Richard, saying, 'there's never a man ... / Can lesser hide his love or hate than he' (lines 51–2) – in other words, you can always tell what Richard is thinking – the audience knows that this is untrue and that Hastings is about to discover it!

CHECKPOINT 8

What does Richard accuse Lord Hastings of? Is his accusation fair in any way?

Hastings's woe

Hastings's final speech, interrupted twice, is a good example of a character's 'last words'. He uses a trio of recollections to illustrate how foolish he has been: he ignored the warning from Lord Stanley, Earl of Derby; he took no notice when it seemed even his horse did not want to take him to the Tower of London; and he gloated when his enemies were executed. He remembers Margaret's curse, and says how foolish it is to trust in men rather than God: whoever does so is like a 'drunken sailor on a mast' who is likely at any moment to fall into the sea and drown (lines 95–100).

Hastings finishes with his own prophecy and curse:

> O bloody Richard! Miserable England!
> I prophesy the fearfull'st time to thee
> That ever wretched age hath looked upon! (lines 102–4)

SCENE 5 – RICHARD TRIES TO WIN THE SUPPORT OF THE PEOPLE

1 The Lord Mayor of London is persuaded that Hastings was a traitor.

2 Richard and Buckingham blacken Edward IV's name and that of his children.

It is important that the citizens of London support Richard's bid for power. Firstly, Richard and Buckingham persuade the Lord Mayor of London of Hastings's treachery. He takes their word for it – 'He deserved his death!' he exclaims finally (line 47) – or perhaps he just pretends to believe them. Secondly, Richard and Buckingham plan to spread lies about the previous king, Edward IV: what a bad character he was and how his sons are illegitimate and therefore not the rightful heirs to the throne.

Spin

Spreading false and exaggerated information about your opponents has always been a tactic used in conflict. There are well-known examples from recent events in this country and around the world. Richard tries to put his own slant or 'spin' on events – we could even call Buckingham his 'spin doctor'. However, we are not sure how far people believe his lies and rumours.

SCENE 6 – A SCRIVENER COMMENTS UPON THE CHARGES AGAINST HASTINGS

1 The scrivener holds a copy of the charges against Lord Hastings.

2 He had already started writing out these charges before Hastings was accused.

We see how people understand what is going on but decide to keep quiet. The scrivener, or legal clerk, says he has just spent eleven hours writing out the charges against the Lord Chamberlain, and it

DID YOU KNOW?

Before the development of democracy (a government which is elected by the people), the only way a king or queen could claim to be the real and legal ruler was through the system called primogeniture – in other words, the firstborn of the previous monarch became the next ruler. This was usually, but not always, restricted to the male line. If there was no male heir, all sorts of more distant relatives might start to claim the throne.

EXAMINER'S SECRET

If you can link what is happening in the play to events or people in the news today, this shows that you have understood the **text**. Keep your comparisons brief, though.

GLOSSARY

fearfull'st most fearful, most dreadful

was given to him to do hours before Hastings was accused of treason. In other words, Hastings's death was illegal. 'Who is so gross / That cannot see this palpable device?' asks the scrivener (lines 10–11).

SCENE 7 – BUCKINGHAM TRIES TO WIN SUPPORT FOR RICHARD

1 **Buckingham's first attempt to win over the crowd is not successful.**

2 **The Lord Mayor and others call on Richard to be king.**

3 **Richard at first refuses, then accepts.**

The Duke of Buckingham reports back to Richard that he spoke to the crowd as he said he would, but they did not respond. Only a few of their own supporters shouted '"God save King Richard!"' (line 36).

Later, Buckingham and Sir William Catesby organise a scene where they, together with the Lord Mayor of London and some important citizens, urge Richard to take the crown. Richard appears with two bishops, reading a prayer book, and refuses. Finally, though, he gives in and agrees to their request: 'Since you will buckle fortune on my back ... / I must have patience to endure the load' (lines 227–9).

> ### Religion
>
> Richard uses the bishops and the prayer book to imply his honesty and goodness. They act as his stage props, and Buckingham calls them 'True ornaments to know a holy man!' (line 98). There are many other religious references in the play. We see very little evidence of real belief, however, and most of the characters become religious only when they are about to die.

CHECKPOINT 9

What strategies does Buckingham use to convince the Lord Mayor and citizens of London that Richard deserves the crown – and Edward IV's sons do not?

GLOSSARY

gross stupid

palpable device obvious trick or lie

ornaments symbols, signs

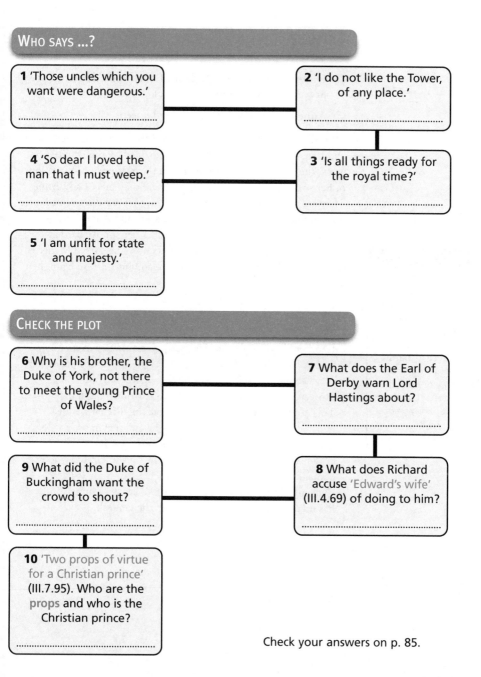

WHO SAYS ...?

1 'Those uncles which you want were dangerous.'

....

2 'I do not like the Tower, of any place.'

....

4 'So dear I loved the man that I must weep.'

....

3 'Is all things ready for the royal time?'

....

5 'I am unfit for state and majesty.'

....

CHECK THE PLOT

6 Why is his brother, the Duke of York, not there to meet the young Prince of Wales?

....

7 What does the Earl of Derby warn Lord Hastings about?

....

9 What did the Duke of Buckingham want the crowd to shout?

....

8 What does Richard accuse 'Edward's wife' (III.4.69) of doing to him?

....

10 'Two props of virtue for a Christian prince' (III.7.95). Who are the **props** and who is the Christian prince?

....

Check your answers on p. 85.

SCENE 1 – RICHARD WILL BE KING; ANNE WILL BE QUEEN

1 Queen Elizabeth, the Duchess of York and Lady Anne are prevented from seeing the princes.

2 Anne is summoned to be crowned queen.

Outside the Tower of London, Queen Elizabeth has come to see her children, the two princes. She is accompanied by the Duchess of York, the children's grandmother; and the Marquis of Dorset, one of her sons from her first marriage. There they meet Lady Anne. They are not allowed in to visit the princes. They discover, to their horror, that Richard is to be crowned king, and Anne must go to be crowned queen. The duchess describes her son Richard as 'murderous' (line 55). Anne remembers how she cursed Richard (Act I Scene 2), and now her curses are coming back to haunt her. The princes remain unvisited.

CHECKPOINT 10

Why do you think Sir Robert Brakenbury makes the slip of calling Richard 'The King' (line 17)? Is it because Richard is behaving like a king – or does the lieutenant of the Tower know more than he is revealing?

Women in *Richard III*

In other Shakespeare plays we see powerful women such as Lady Macbeth, or Queen Margaret as she appears in the earlier plays about King Henry VI (the three parts of *Henry VI*). However, in this play, none of the four women has much power. This does not stop them verbally attacking Richard, other characters and one another; but in the end they must go along with events, run away or hide. Anne does not want to be crowned queen, but has no choice. She says to Derby, who has come to fetch her, 'I with all unwillingness will go' (line 57). Queen Elizabeth, refused permission to see her young sons, has no choice but to seek safety with the Church.

SCENE 2 – RICHARD WANTS THE YOUNG PRINCES KILLED

❶ Buckingham fails to help Richard in his wish to have the princes killed, and Richard is furious.

❷ The Earl of Richmond is gathering an army against Richard.

❸ Buckingham, failing to gain any reward for his services to Richard, decides to join Richmond.

Richard is king! But he still does not feel secure. He wants his nephews the Prince of Wales (Edward V) and the Duke of York killed and he wants Buckingham to agree to help him. Richard is also testing Buckingham to see if he is 'current gold' (line 9). In reply, Buckingham asks for time to think, and leaves. Richard is not pleased, and vows that Buckingham 'No more shall be the neighbour to my counsels' (line 43). He makes contact with Tyrrel, 'a discontented gentleman' (line 36) who will do anything for money, including killing the two princes. Buckingham returns, saying he has thought about Richard's request, but Richard will not listen to him.

CHECKPOINT 11

How should Buckingham deliver his lines in the first part of this scene? Should the actor show the 'ice' that Richard mentions (line 22), or try to appear friendly and supportive? What other ways might there be?

DID YOU KNOW?

Marrying Princess Elizabeth, daughter of Edward IV and Queen Elizabeth and sister of the two princes, would help Richard strengthen his grip on the throne. Any child of theirs would have a very strong claim to inherit the crown of England.

Events begin to move swiftly. News comes that the Earl of Richmond, one of the most important men opposing Richard – who has his own possible claim to the throne – is gathering an army. Richard puts out a rumour that his wife, Anne, is sick. He now plans to marry his niece, Princess Elizabeth, which will make his position as king more secure. Buckingham departs, having failed to gain his reward and fearing for his life.

> **The rewards of loyalty**
>
> Buckingham asks for his reward, which Richard promised him earlier for his support and help (III.1.194–6), but Richard retorts, 'I am not in the giving vein today' (line 116). He expects Buckingham to agree to his every wish and demand, and when Buckingham refuses to do so, this one instance of independence is enough to make Richard turn against him.
>
> Buckingham realises that all his support has been for nothing. Richard has no use for anyone who cannot – or will not – help him get what he wants. 'Made I him King for *this*?' thinks Buckingham (line 120). 'O, let me think on Hastings, and be gone … / while my fearful head is on!' (lines 121–2).

Scene 3 – The young princes are dead but armies are gathering

1. **The princes have been murdered in the Tower of London.**

2. **Queen Anne is dead and Richard plans to marry Princess Elizabeth.**

3. **Richard's enemies are increasing.**

The Prince of Wales (Edward V) and his younger brother, the Duke of York, have been murdered in the Tower of London. Even Tyrrel could not do it personally and calls it a 'piece of ruthful butchery' (line 5). Richard is pleased, though, and ticks off a kind of list:

- The Duke of Clarence's son is 'pent up' (line 36).

- Clarence's daughter has been married to someone of no importance.

- Edward IV's sons are dead.

- Queen Anne 'hath bid this world good night' (line 39) – how she has died, we do not know.

- The Earl of Richmond plans to marry Princess Elizabeth, Edward IV and Queen Elizabeth's daughter, but her uncle Richard aims to get there first.

In something like a newsflash we hear that the Bishop of Ely has joined Richmond and that Buckingham has also joined Richard's enemies.

Latest news

As events move towards a climax, the audience is informed of them in brief announcements. These are like newsflashes or the 'breaking news' which we see on television. Usually a messenger rushes on stage, reports the latest events and leaves. Here it is Sir Richard Ratcliffe, one of Richard's supporters, who uses just three lines (46–8) to deliver his 'Bad news'.

? DID YOU KNOW?

In the Middle Ages, bishops often had considerable political power and ruled large areas of land. Some, like the Bishop of Ely, would have been able to raise armies and even lead them into battle.

SCENE 4 – THE WOMEN GRIEVE, RICHARD CONSIDERS A NEW WIFE AND ENEMIES BEGIN TO GATHER

1 The women grieve for their murdered relatives and curse Richard.

2 Richard seeks Queen Elizabeth's help to woo her daughter.

3 The Earl of Richmond is on his way to England.

In the first part of this long scene, Queen Elizabeth is grieving for her murdered sons. She is accompanied by the Duchess of York, and they are joined by Queen Margaret. All express their grief, and

GLOSSARY

vein mood

ruthful ruthless, pitiless

pent up imprisoned

> ### CHECKPOINT 12
>
> Queen Margaret uses a wide range of curses and insults for Richard. What other animals does she compare him to? Look especially in Act I Scene 3.

all blame Richard. 'From forth the kennel of thy womb hath crept / A hell-hound that doth hunt us all to death!' says Margaret to the duchess (lines 47–8). Margaret is pleased about the deaths of those who killed her family, and is delighted that her prophecies and curses have come true.

The duchess and Elizabeth resolve to curse Richard as forcefully as Margaret does, and when Richard enters 'marching with soldiers' (after line 135) they do their best with **phrases** such as 'villain slave!' and 'thou toad!' (lines 144 and 145). The duchess's last words to her only remaining son are 'Bloody thou art. Bloody will be thy end!' (line 195).

> ### CHECKPOINT 13
>
> What arguments does Richard use to convince Queen Elizabeth that she should support his courtship of her daughter? Why might she agree?

In the second part, we see Richard trying to win Queen Elizabeth's help to woo her daughter, Elizabeth. In the long exchange between them she keeps reminding him of the evil he has done, and he keeps replying in a soothing manner. He says he will make it up to her daughter by making her queen: 'If I did take the kingdom from your sons, / To make amends I'll give it to your daughter' (lines 294–5). Richard also says it is the only way to bring peace to England. Elizabeth does not commit herself, but Richard thinks he has won her over when he says: 'Relenting fool, and shallow, changing woman!' (line 431).

Once again, reports of the gathering enemy forces now build up like a series of newsflashes. The Earl of Richmond is heading for England, 'here to claim the crown' (line 468). The news is mainly bad – the rebels' 'power grows strong' (line 505). One piece of good news, however, is that the Duke of Buckingham has been captured.

> #### Richard unsure
>
> For the first time we see Richard when he is not in control. Things are getting out of hand and he is no longer the cunning manipulator of people and events. In the exchanges following line 440 he gives half-thought-out orders and seems distracted and confused. 'My mind is changed' he says to Sir Richard Ratcliffe in a moment of uncertainty (line 456). Later he loses his temper and strikes one of the messengers.

SCENE 5 – MORE FORCES GATHER

1 The Earl of Derby supports the Earl of Richmond.

2 Princess Elizabeth will marry Richmond.

This scene also acts as a newsflash from a different angle. We learn of more forces gathering against Richard; that Lord Stanley, the Earl of Derby, is secretly on Richmond's side; and that Queen Elizabeth has agreed to let her daughter, Princess Elizabeth, marry Richmond.

GLOSSARY
Relenting Forgiving

WHO SAYS ...?

1 'Ah, cut my lace asunder!'

....

2 'Pity, you ancient stones, those tender babes'

....

4 'Infer fair England's peace by this alliance.'

....

3 'The tyrannous and bloody act is done'

....

5 'He makes for England here to claim the crown.'

....

CHECK THE PLOT

6 Who does Elizabeth ask for help to curse Richard?

....

7 Why is Richard angry with the Duke of Buckingham?

....

9 What reasons does Richard give for wanting to marry Princess Elizabeth?

....

8 Why does Buckingham abandon Richard?

....

10 Why can't the Earl of Derby commit himself to the Earl of Richmond's side?

....

Check your answers on p. 86.

SCENE 1 – THE END OF BUCKINGHAM

1 Buckingham is refused permission to speak to Richard.

2 Buckingham is then led towards his execution.

As he is led to his execution, the Duke of Buckingham recognises the evil he has done. He doesn't blame anyone else, and accepts that another of Margaret's curses has come true. 'Thus Margaret's curse falls heavy on my neck' (line 25) – as will the axe. In Act II Scene 1 (lines 32–40) he pledged loyalty to Queen Elizabeth, asking to be punished by God if he was false. Here he remembers his broken promise and finds it fitting that it is on All Souls' Day, when people prayed for the souls of the dead, that he is so punished.

SCENE 2 – RICHMOND'S POWER GROWS

1 Richmond gives a rousing speech to his men.

2 He promises peace.

The Earl of Richmond has advanced into the kingdom. His army will soon face Richard's in battle. In a rousing speech to his supporters, in which he calls Richard 'The wretched ... usurping boar' (line 7), Richmond urges them to fight 'In God's name' for 'perpetual peace' (lines 14 and 15). One of his followers says that Richard 'hath no friends but what are friends for fear' (line 20).

> **CHECKPOINT 14**
>
> What does the fact that Richmond has marched all the way to the Midlands without being challenged tell us?

SCENE 3 – THE BATTLE FOR THE CROWN OF ENGLAND

1 Richard and Richmond prepare for battle.

2 They are both visited by the ghosts of those killed by Richard.

3 Richard and Richmond address their troops.

4 The Earl of Derby will not bring his men to support Richard.

> **GLOSSARY**
>
> **wretched** loathsome
>
> **usurping** illegally crowned
>
> **perpetual** everlasting

Having arrived at Bosworth, Richard makes plans for battle. Near by, the Earl of Richmond is doing the same. Both men then rest. In their sleep they are visited by the ghosts of those killed by Richard. These ghosts praise Richmond and curse Richard, each ending their speech to him with the words 'Despair and die!' On waking, Richard confesses how these dreams have affected him more than 'the substance of ten thousand soldiers' (line 218). Richmond, however, has slept well.

Both leaders give inspiring speeches to their troops. At the last moment, Richard learns that Lord Stanley, Earl of Derby, will not come to his support.

CHECKPOINT 15

Both Richmond and Richard call upon the same saint for help. Which one, and why?

> **Inspiring speeches**
>
> Shakespeare's audiences would have responded enthusiastically to passionate speeches. In this scene Richmond's speech to his troops is a classic of its kind (lines 237–70). Notice how he uses repetition. He mentions God six times and attaches words like 'good', 'prayers', 'saints', 'justice' and 'peace' to his own side. He dwells on the evil of their enemy, 'A bloody tyrant and a homicide! / One raised in blood, and one in blood established' (lines 246–7). More repetition occurs where he uses the form 'If you …' in four ringing sentences one after the other (lines 255–62), and he ends with a series of bold and cheerful exclamations.

> **Ghosts**
>
> Ghosts are often found in Shakespeare's plays. Like dreams, ghosts can be used to bring out the hidden emotions of a character. How would you indicate that an actor was playing a ghost rather than a normal character?

SCENE 4 – THE BATTLE OF BOSWORTH

① **The battle begins.**

② **Richard tries to find and kill Richmond.**

Richard fights bravely, even after his horse has been killed. 'A horse! A horse! My kingdom for a horse!' (line 7) is one of the most famous lines from Shakespeare. However, he fails to locate Richmond, despite managing to kill five soldiers who look like his opponent.

> ### Battles
>
> The acting area of the Globe Theatre was not large, but Shakespeare had no hesitation in writing battle scenes for its stage. In *Richard III* the stage directions in Act V Scene 3 require that Richard's army is camped out on one side of the stage and Richmond's on the other. The battle itself shifts to 'The centre of the battlefield' in Act V Scene 5. Directors have to think very carefully about the most effective ways to show the actions of battle on a stage.

DID YOU KNOW?

In battle several soldiers would often be dressed like the king to confuse the enemy. Richard exclaims, **'I think there be six Richmonds in the field. / Five have I slain today instead of him!'** (lines 11–12). However wicked Richard might be, no one can doubt his bravery.

SCENE 5 – RICHARD IS DEFEATED

① **Richard is killed.**

② **Richmond accepts the crown of England.**

Finally Richard and Richmond confront each other on the battlefield. In the fight, Richard is killed. The crown is 'plucked off' Richard's head by the Earl of Derby and handed to Richmond (line 6), who announces his intention to marry Princess Elizabeth. He hopes that his reign and this marriage, which 'will unite the white rose and the red' (line 19), will bring an end to civil war in England.

DID YOU KNOW?

Richard III was the third and last English king to die in battle; he was only thirty-two at the time.

GLOSSARY

substance reality, solid presence

homicide murderer

Now take a break!

WHO SAYS ...?

1 'Come lead me, officers, to the block of shame!'

....

2 'True hope is swift and flies with swallow's wings'

....

4 'God and good angels fight on Richmond's side'

....

3 'Think on the Tower and me.'

....

5 'The bloody dog is dead.'

....

CHECK THE PLOT

6 What does Sir James Blunt say about Richard's supporters?

....

7 How many ghosts appear to Richard and Richmond?

....

9 What is Richard's personal aim on the battlefield?

....

8 What effect do the ghosts appear to have on Richard?

....

10 How will Richmond link the houses of York and Lancaster?

....

Check your answers on p. 86.

PART THREE

CHARACTER AND MOTIVATION

RICHARD

Unlike some other great characters that Shakespeare created, such as Macbeth or Othello, Richard's character is not double-sided or mysterious. He is presented as a villain and he behaves like a villain. He says he will perform evil deeds and he does.

Shakespeare is direct with the audience from the start. Richard's speech to us at the very beginning of the play states that he is 'determinèd to prove a villain' (I.1.30). He places the blame for his evil nature on the fact that he was born 'Deformed, unfinished' (I.1.20) and so loathsome that 'dogs bark at me as I halt by them' (I.1.23). Although he is being honest with the audience, there is some exaggeration here. He has a successful history as a soldier, brave and ruthless, and clearly is not repulsive to women – in spite of what he says.

Villainous
Cunning
Brave

On the surface, there is little about Richard that should make the audience feel sympathetic towards him. At most, we should appreciate his willpower, his ability with words and his skill in managing people and events. Many politicians and almost all dictators share these talents. His motives appear to be power for its own sake, together with pleasure in the destruction of all those who have, he feels, looked down on him. However, audiences will sometimes warm to a villain, and Richard is undoubtedly a magnetic character. Whenever he is on stage, he controls events, and his wicked asides are often very funny. His cheerful confessions of his own trickery, together with the pleasure he receives from controlling his enemies, are fascinating. It is almost impossible not to be affected by his forceful personality.

Except when he talks directly to the audience, we cannot expect anything Richard says to be true. The first person he speaks to is his brother George, Duke of Clarence, whose death he is plotting.

He tells Clarence: 'I will deliver you' (I.1.115) – and goes off to do the opposite. One of his next actions is to marry Lady Anne, not because he loves her, but because it will help him on the road to power. This cruel coldness is typical of him throughout the play.

Richard can act a part to achieve a goal. He pretends remorse to Lady Anne in the scene where he presents her with his sword for her to kill him (Act I Scene 2), and to Queen Elizabeth when he wants to win her daughter. He pretends to be religious when the citizens appeal to him to be king (Act III Scene 7), and he pretends to be angry at being misjudged. In Act I Scene 3, for example, he accuses Elizabeth and her relatives Lord Grey and Earl Rivers of spreading rumours about him, when it is he who has been telling lies about them (line 42 onwards)!

However, as events move on, it becomes clear that fewer and fewer people believe or trust Richard. By the end of the play he has few followers. Those who stay with him do so mainly out of fear. At the end, he has nothing, not even a horse, and when he dies, no one will be sorry. After all his careful plotting he is finally content to let luck decide his fate: 'I have set my life upon a cast / And I will stand the hazard of the die' (V.4.9–10).

BUCKINGHAM

The Duke of Buckingham plays a small part in the first act and appears as just one of many nobles and courtiers. We only gradually realise that he is Richard's closest supporter. Richard calls him 'My other self' (II.2.151), and throughout the remainder of Act II and Act III we see him plotting with Richard to acquire the crown. He does not just carry out Richard's orders but has plenty of his own. It is Buckingham who organises the bringing of the young Prince of Wales quietly to London. It is Buckingham who plots and carries out the manipulation of the Lord Mayor of London and the citizens in Act III Scene 7.

There seems to be no greater motive for his actions than a desire for power and an enjoyment of conspiracy for its own sake. He has no concerns about arranging the killing of those who stand in Richard's way. Like Richard, he sees others as pawns in their own game.

Clever
Persuasive
Cunning

GLOSSARY

cast throw of the dice

stand accept

hazard chance, luck

He hesitates – 'Give me some little breath, some pause' (IV.2.24) – when it comes to the murder of the two princes. However, we never know what his final response might have been, as Richard interrupts him before he can reveal what he thinks. His hesitation is enough to turn Richard against him. Buckingham immediately realises that Richard will get rid of him as easily as he disposed of others. 'Repays he my deep service / With such contempt?' he says, as he goes over to the Earl of Richmond's side (IV.2.119–20). We might wonder how loyal he would be to anyone, but no doubt Richmond would welcome any help at this point.

When Buckingham is captured and executed, it is hard to have much sympathy for him. But, unlike many others, he does not complain or cast blame. He recognises that he has done wrong and he deserves his punishment: 'Wrong hath but wrong' (V.1.29).

ANNE

Lady Anne is the widow of Edward, the son of King Henry VI. Both men were killed by Richard in the Wars of the Roses. No wonder then that she curses Richard as a 'dreadful minister of hell!' (I.2.46) and a 'lump of foul deformity' (I.2.57), and spits at him (I.2.145). However, by the end of Act I Scene 2, Richard has persuaded Anne to wear his ring and, it seems, convinced Anne that he loves her.

Angry
Gullible
Vulnerable

How can we explain Anne's behaviour? Perhaps the best way to understand is to put ourselves in her position. She is alone and defenceless. Her options are to flee the country or seek refuge with someone who can protect her. Perhaps her best chance of survival lies with this strong (and oddly charming) man. Richard himself can hardly believe his success: 'Was ever woman in this humour won?' (I.2.229).

We do not meet Anne again until just before the coronation. She has married Richard but it brings her no comfort or safety. She admits she 'grew captive to his honey words' (IV.1.79), but that now she is to be crowned queen she would rather the gold crown was made of 'red-hot steel, to sear me to the brains!' (IV.1.60). She goes on: 'he hates me ... / And will, no doubt, shortly be rid of me' (IV.1.85–6). How right she is.

ELIZABETH

Queen Elizabeth is the wife of King Edward IV and mother of the two young princes (the Prince of Wales and the Duke of York – the heirs to the throne). She has a daughter by the king, also called Elizabeth. Her family is powerful and its influence is resented by others, especially Richard. Her brother, Earl Rivers, and her two sons from her earlier marriage, the Marquis of Dorset and Lord Grey, all play a significant role in the drama.

Elizabeth, knowing her husband, Edward IV, is sick, fears what will happen if he dies: 'If he were dead, what would betide on me?' (I.3.6). She realises that Richard doesn't like her, and is direct when she speaks to him: 'You envy my advancement and my friends' (I.3.74). She resents the way rumours have been started (by Richard, of course) that she is responsible for the Duke of Clarence being accused and imprisoned: 'I had rather be a country servant-maid / Than a great queen ... so baited, scorned, and stormed at' (I.3.106–8).

Intelligent
Cautious
Loyal

When the death of her husband occurs, her fears prove correct. Almost immediately, two of her family, Earl Rivers and Lord Grey, are arrested and executed. 'I see the ruin of my house!' she cries, '... destruction, blood, and massacre!' (II.4.50–4). Shortly afterwards her young sons the princes are taken away from her and she is prevented from seeing them. She urges her remaining son, Dorset, to flee – 'hie thee from this slaughter-house!' (IV.1.43) – after receiving the 'dead-killing news' that Richard is to be king (IV.1.35). When her sons the princes are murdered, Queen Elizabeth joins Queen Margaret and the Duchess of York in both grieving for the various victims of the struggle for power and in cursing her enemies.

Richard adds to Elizabeth's troubles by asking for her help in marrying her daughter. The audience shares her reaction of amazement and repulsion. 'How canst *thou* woo her?' she asks (IV.4.268). It is not clear what she means when she leaves, promising to get back to Richard about his offer. It may be that she can stand him no longer and has already decided that her daughter will marry the Earl of Richmond.

Bitter

Unforgiving

Proud

MARGARET

Margaret is called Queen Margaret in some editions of the play. This is because she was queen of England when her husband, the Lancastrian Henry VI, was king. Her son, Edward, was Prince of Wales and heir to the throne. In the course of the wars between the houses of Lancaster and York (the Wars of the Roses), both her husband and her son were killed. For these deaths, she holds not only Richard responsible, but all the other Yorkists. She accuses them of being 'standers by' when her son was murdered (I.3.209).

Margaret has been a very powerful woman in her time, but now she is bitter not just because of the killing of her husband and son but also because of her own loss of power. She hates almost all of the other nobles and courtiers in England and curses them whenever she meets them. Yet they put up with her presence because she is harmless.

Margaret reserves her most violent curses for Richard, 'the son of hell' (I.3.229). She calls him, among other things, a 'bottled spider' (I.3.241), a 'poisonous bunch-backed toad!' (I.3.245) and a 'hell-hound' (IV.4.48). She also resents Queen Elizabeth for taking her place, which she still thinks she deserves.

Margaret's curses are mixed with prophecies about the death and destruction of those around her. As the play progresses, she relishes each moment when another of her enemies dies. The others, too, remember her curses. 'Now Margaret's curse is fall'n upon our heads' (III.3.14) says Lord Grey on his way to execution; and Lord Hastings, in the next scene, cries, 'Margaret, now thy heavy curse / Is lighted on poor Hastings' wretched head!' (III.4.91–2).

CLARENCE

George, Duke of Clarence, brother to Edward IV and Richard, has played his part in the struggle for power but is shown in *Richard III* as gentle and trusting. He believes his younger brother Richard is on his side. He can do nothing against Richard's plotting or the brutal strength of the first murderer. His dream (or nightmare) shows his anxiety about what will happen to him while he is alive and after he is dead. It also tells the audience that he is not the innocent character he might otherwise seem: 'I have done these things / That now give evidence against my soul' (I.4.66–7). In other words, the bad deeds he has done in his life have now come back to haunt him.

EDWARD IV

The new king, Edward IV, husband of Queen Elizabeth, has gained the throne by war, yet he does not seem a very strong ruler. He is an ill man at the start of the play – in Act I Scene 3 we see Elizabeth worrying about his health, and what will happen after his death. England under his rule does not seem settled or particularly peaceful. Although he tries to put an end to the quarrelling at court, Edward does not realise that Richard is to blame for making the divisions worse. In fact, Edward is completely fooled by his brother, and does not recognise Richard's ambition or true nature. His decision to send his brother Clarence to the Tower of London because of a prophecy makes him appear weak and superstitious, and his judgement seem poor.

DUCHESS OF YORK

The Duchess of York is the mother of Edward, Clarence and Richard. She grieves for her two older sons, suspecting that Richard – her 'damnèd son' (IV.4.134) – is to blame for Clarence's death: 'thou toad! – where is thy brother Clarence?' (IV.4.145). She recognises Richard's villainy but is powerless to do anything about it. This does not stop her often cursing him violently.

RICHMOND

The Earl of Richmond is able to challenge Richard for the throne because he is connected to the house of Lancaster. As a focus for the forces opposed to Richard, Richmond is presented as noble, honest and the complete opposite of the 'tyrant' (V.3.246). On Richard's death in battle he becomes Henry VII, the first Tudor king.

DID YOU KNOW?

Richard III is Shakespeare's second longest play. *Hamlet* is the longest.

DERBY

Lord Stanley, Earl of Derby, is Richmond's stepfather and is not trusted by Richard. Derby recognises the danger Richard poses from early on and tries to warn Hastings, but Hastings refuses to listen. Derby secretly supports Richmond but only brings his troops into the battle on Richmond's side at the last minute, because Richard is holding his son as a hostage.

HASTINGS

Lord Hastings is the Lord Chamberlain, who would have had considerable power at the time of the play. He is an honest man who serves Edward IV and will not support Richard as king, even though he trusts him. He cannot see the danger he is in, believing that Richard 'loves me well' (III.4.14), and as a result is arrested for 'treason' and executed.

RIVERS, DORSET AND GREY

These nobles are relations ('kinsmen') of Queen Elizabeth. Earl Rivers is her brother; the Marquis of Dorset and Lord Grey are her sons from her previous marriage. They are resented by Richard and other courtiers for having too much power. Richard has Rivers and Grey executed, but Dorset escapes and joins Richmond's rebellion.

CATESBY

Sir William Catesby is Richard's unthinking servant and ally. He is prepared to hire child-murderers and spy on those who trust him. However, he remains loyal to Richard until the very end. Indeed, he is the last person to speak to him, in Act V Scene 4, when Richard is losing the battle: 'Withdraw, my lord! I'll help you to a horse' (line 8).

DID YOU KNOW?

Elizabeth Woodville (later Queen Elizabeth) was first married to Sir John Grey, who later died. Her marriage to Edward IV was unpopular with the nobles of England because she was not high-born, and Edward made things worse when he treated a number of her relatives favourably.

IDEAS, THEMES AND ISSUES

LIES AND DECEPTIONS

This theme is concerned with how things *appear* compared to how they *actually are*, in other words 'appearance and reality'. It is a common theme in Shakespeare. The stage gives actors the opportunity to say one thing to the audience and something different to the other characters. Sometimes it might be just a look that Richard, for instance, gives to the audience that says 'What I'm saying is a pack of lies – and you know it!'

It is Richard who deceives people most, of course, though Buckingham and one or two others do their share. Buckingham tells Richard in Act III Scene 5 that he too 'can counterfeit the deep tragedian!' and put on different expressions (line 5). In other words, he's good at acting as well!

Richard's actions throughout the play depend on a series of lies and deceptions, beginning with his conversation with his brother Clarence. When Clarence is about to be murdered, he is still convinced that Richard is on his side because he 'swore with sobs / That he would labour my delivery' (I.4.233–4). Richard's lies continue through the scene where Edward is attempting to make peace between the different groups at court (Act II Scene 1). If he has done anything to offend anyone, he says, 'I desire / To reconcile me to his friendly peace' (II.1.59–60). His appearance as the kindly uncle to the young princes is both sickening and horrible (Act III Scene 1).

Some characters are easily deceived, such as Lord Hastings and the Lord Mayor of London. Others are less easily fooled. The Duchess of York, Richard's mother, who knows him all too well, and Margaret have no doubts about his true character. The duchess says angrily to her son that he has brought her nothing but hurt and suffering since he was born: 'Thou cam'st on earth to make the earth my hell!' (IV.4.167). Sometimes we do not know whether Richard deceives or not. Is he sincere when he promises Buckingham the earldom of Hereford (Act III Scene 1)? Can we ever believe him when he expresses remorse for the murders he has done?

We see deception elsewhere, but never as strongly. Buckingham deceives the citizens and the Lord Mayor into believing Richard is a religious man who does not want the stress of ruling the country. Indeed, Buckingham deceives most people into thinking he is himself an honest servant of the people. Sir William Catesby

> **CHECKPOINT 16**
>
> Are there any instances where you think the audience is really likely to be fooled by Richard?

> **GLOSSARY**
>
> **counterfeit** fake
>
> **deep tragedian** actor good at playing tragic roles
>
> **labour my delivery** work to set me free

deceives Hastings in order to find out his true feelings, and Derby tries to keep Richard believing he is loyal in order to protect his son.

Throughout the play, however, reality keeps breaking through. The scrivener makes this clear with his speech in Act III Scene 6: 'Bad is the world … / When such ill dealing must be seen in thought' (lines 13–14) – in other words, everyone knows what's going on but they can only think it, not say it.

THE POSITION OF WOMEN

Shakespeare gives a lot of time and many lines to the women in the play. The number of speeches they have far outweighs the effect they have on events. Nevertheless, they are important characters and provide a commentary on what is going on that is very different from the viewpoint of most of the male characters.

The four women in the play – Elizabeth, Anne, Margaret and the Duchess of York – have all had power at some point, but all have lost it or lose it during the play. In spite of their lack of power, the women often have influence. It is important to Richard, for instance, to marry the young Princess Elizabeth and thus unite the country. He tells Queen Elizabeth, the princess's mother: 'Death, desolation, ruin, and decay. / It cannot be avoided but by this' (IV.4.409–10).

Dreadful things happen to their families, so it is not surprising that the women in the play spend time grieving and cursing. 'Cursed be the hand that made these fatal holes! / Cursed the heart that had the heart to do it!' cries Anne, speaking over her father-in-law's corpse (I.2.14–15). 'Ah, my poor princes! Ah, my tender babes!' wails Elizabeth, grieving for her murdered sons (IV.4.9).

While the play is about national politics and war, it is mostly through families that we see the events happen. The emotional reactions of the female characters show us that war and conflict have a human cost, through the death of sons, fathers, brothers and husbands.

CHECKPOINT 17

Are there any events the women in the play do influence?

DID YOU KNOW?

The real Margaret of Anjou was indeed the former queen of England, and widow of Henry VI. However, in reality she had retired to France by the time the events in *Richard III* take place, and died before Richard became king.

FORTUNE'S UPS AND DOWNS

Changes in characters' fortunes are a major theme in Shakespeare's plays. Elizabethan audiences would have been familiar with the idea of a 'wheel of fortune'. It was a common feeling that success in life was often followed by failure, good things by bad and bad things by good. In the case of those in power, people were even more interested in their ups and downs, and there was a certain satisfaction in seeing the powerful lose their power and status. Today we can see how the media, particularly some newspapers, love to see a hero brought low.

In the case of someone like Richard, there is an extra satisfaction in seeing the downfall of such an evil man. Richard's rise is slow and unstoppable, while his fall is very fast. Others in the play also suffer from changing fortunes. Some deserve it, like Buckingham; and others, like Lord Hastings, do not. We are also reminded by the female characters, especially Margaret, the former queen, how they themselves once had influence and status but now have almost none.

On the other hand, we see Richmond's fortunes rise. He begins as someone of only minor importance, it seems, and ends up the heroic and victorious figure of the final scene. Are you surprised that he emerges as the most important character at the end? Should he have been given more status in the first half of the play?

The fortunes of the country are bound up with that of its rulers. Therefore Hastings mourns not just his own fate but that of 'Miserable England!' (III.4.102). Richard's rise to power is not just a nightmare for his opponents but for the country as a whole. His downfall brings a sense of deliverance for the whole kingdom.

CONSCIENCE

Conscience is our own sense of what is right and wrong. It is a powerful force and often affects our behaviour. Feelings of conscience are most obvious in the characters of the murderers of the Duke of Clarence. Their comic exchanges in Act I Scene 4 cannot hide the fact that they are uneasy. The first murderer can ignore his conscience; the second cannot: 'I repent me that the Duke

> **CHECKPOINT 18**
>
> Can you think of examples of modern-day heroes being brought down? You may also be able to find examples in literature, including traditional stories and fairy tales.

> **GLOSSARY**
>
> **ill dealing** wicked acts
> **repent me** am sorry

DID YOU KNOW?
'Every man's conscience is a thousand men' says Richmond's ally, the Earl of Oxford (V.2.17), meaning that each man in Richmond's army, because they are acting in the right way, with good on their side, is made a thousand times stronger. This exaggeration contains a truth: that men will fight more bravely if they believe their cause is just.

is slain' (line 267). Even the murderers of the princes, who must be more thick-skinned than most, show some signs of humanity: 'With conscience and remorse / They could not speak' (IV.3.20–1). Buckingham, too, seems to hesitate when it comes to such a dreadful murder, though we never learn whether he has overcome his conscience or not.

Richard is very disturbed by the visits of the ghosts of his murdered victims. As the play nears its end, the guilt of all the lies and murders gathers on his shoulders: 'My conscience hath a thousand several tongues' (V.3.193). He tries to throw off these feelings of conscience and remorse, claiming 'Conscience is but a word that cowards use' (V.3.309). At the end, Richard shows no sign of conscience, preferring to risk everything in the battle. Do we have any sympathy for him at all? If we do not, is Richard too simple a character, a symbol of evil rather than a real, fully rounded person?

THE LANGUAGE OF THE TEXT

RISE AND FALL

It is interesting to compare Richard's speech at the beginning of the play with his speech near the end (in Act V Scene 3).

His soliloquy in Act I Scene 1 is full of clever images and phrases, beginning with a metaphor taken from the weather:

> Now is the winter of our discontent
> Made glorious summer by this son of York –
> And all the clouds that loured upon our house
> In the deep bosom of the ocean buried. (I.1.1–4)

Bad times are now replaced by good times and the sun has replaced the clouds. As well as the clear imagery, there is the pun of 'son' and 'sun' (see the summary of Act I Scene 1).

There follows a series of swift, neat contrasts: weapons have become souvenirs, calls to battle have become 'merry meetings' and marches have changed to dances (I.1.6–8). Then he creates a personification of war ('Grim-visaged … wrinkled'), who changes from someone frightening into a dancing entertainer – someone who 'capers nimbly' to a 'lute' (I.1.9 and I.1.12–13).

After this careful scene setting, there is a dramatic about-turn. All that he has said so far seems positive and admirable. But not for Richard! He contrasts himself with the dancing entertainer, exaggerating all his worst features. He brings this speech to a climax with the startling revelation that he is 'determinèd to prove a villain' and 'hate the idle pleasures of these days' (I.1.30–1).

Compare this masterful speech with Richard's soliloquy in Act V Scene 3 (lines 177–206). It is almost empty of imagery. There is only the dreadful picture of his conscience with a 'thousand ... tongues' crying '"Guilty! guilty!"' (V.3.193 and V.3.199). Together with this lack of imagery, there are no puns and there is no wit. There is no sign of the long and careful sentences or clever phrases of the earlier speech. There are only five sentences in the first thirty-one lines of Richard's first speech. This isn't because Richard doesn't know how to speak in proper sentences. It is because he is good at expressing and developing his thoughts. In this later speech he is not. In thirty lines there are more than thirty sentences! It is a speech full of questions, exclamations and contradictions. 'Is there a murderer here? No! – yes, I am' (V.3.184).

In fact, this later speech is not addressed to the audience but to himself, and there are few ideas to develop. Richard is rambling and confused. Only rarely does he develop a thought, as in:

> My conscience hath a thousand several tongues,
> And every tongue brings in a several tale,
> And every tale condemns me for a villain. (V.3.193–5)

The confusion of his feelings is further underlined by the rhythm of the lines. The rhythm of the lines in the Act I speech is steady and controlled. In the Act V speech the rhythm is jagged and awkward.

By comparing the two speeches, we see how Richard's language reflects what is happening to him. As his situation has got worse, so has his command of words!

EXAMINER'S SECRET

Try reading a few lines aloud from each speech and see if you can hear the difference between them. Reading the words out loud can give you important clues about the meanings and will bring the **text** alive!

GLOSSARY

several separate, different

loured brooded, frowned

house family

Grim-visaged Stern-faced

IMAGERY

Richard III is not as rich in imagery as many other Shakespeare plays, but there are some images and metaphors that keep cropping up. There are many references to heaven and hell. Richard is called 'the son of hell' (I.3.229), 'damnèd' (IV.4.134), a 'devil' (I.3.117) and a 'cacodemon' (I.3.143). His enemy, 'princely' Richmond, on the other hand (IV.5.9), fights 'in God's name' (V.2.22) and uses lots of biblical images in his speeches. More than one of the ghosts who visit Richmond on the night before the battle call upon 'good angels' to watch over him (Act V Scene 3).

There are also many animal images in *Richard III*. Richard is compared with dogs, boars, spiders, toads and hogs – and usually the adjectives describing these animals are vicious and unpleasant. He is called a 'hell-hound' (IV.4.48), a 'wretched, bloody, and usurping boar' (V.2.7), a 'bottled spider' (I.3.241), and an 'abortive, rooting hog' (I.3.227). When Anne spits at him in Act I Scene 2, she hisses: 'Never hung poison on a fouler toad' (I.2.148).

DID YOU KNOW?

Later in Act V we find Richmond using an extended animal metaphor as he compares Richard to the boar, whose emblem Richard has adopted. This beast 'Swills your warm blood like wash, and makes his trough / In your embowelled bosoms' (V.2.9–10). Richard, he is saying, is like a bloodthirsty animal that drinks your blood.

In *Richard III* there are examples of both simple comparisons and more extended metaphors. One example of a simple comparison is this simile where Buckingham is talking of the citizens, who were 'like dumb statues or breathing stones': they resembled people but were as silent as statues or stones (III.7.25). Later in the same scene, Buckingham uses a more extended image when he compares England to a human body: 'The noble isle doth want her proper limbs – / Her face defaced with scars of infamy' (III.7.124–5). He and Richard are the most likely to use such language. Richard, for example, pretends to turn down the throne because he is 'a bark to brook no mighty sea' (III.7.161) – in other words, he is not a strong enough ship to withstand the dangers of the ocean (leading the country).

Of the other characters, Queen Elizabeth is perhaps the most likely to spice her words with images. When she talks of the Tower of London, her use of imagery takes the form of a metaphor as she describes the prison as a:

> Rough cradle for such little pretty ones.
> Rude ragged nurse, old sullen playfellow
> For tender princes ... (IV.1.100–2)

When she discovers her sons are dead, she calls them her 'unblown flowers, new-appearing sweets!' (IV.4.10): in other words, her young sons were like flowers that had not yet bloomed, and were just appearing as new buds.

INSULTS

Margaret is famous for her curses and her insults; but it is Anne, often seen as a gentle character, who is the first to vent her feelings, when she insults Richard in Act I Scene 2. 'Avaunt, thou dreadful minister of hell!' (line 46), 'diffused infection of a man' (line 78), 'devilish slave' (line 90) and 'unfit for any place but hell!' (line 109) are just a few examples!

Margaret is scathing towards everyone, but she reserves her greatest insults for Richard, as in the much-quoted 'elvish-marked, abortive, rooting hog!' (I.3.227) and 'poisonous bunch-backed toad!' (I.3.245). The same scene contains a wonderful heaping of insults, ending only when she is finally interrupted (at line 233). Richard himself is not to be outdone: 'Have done thy charm, thou hateful withered hag!' he snarls back at Margaret (I.3.214).

Queen Elizabeth is not good at insults. She borrows Margaret's own words and asks for her help to 'curse' Richard (IV.4.80). But even so, Elizabeth's exchanges with Richard after this show her grief rather than her anger. She can be sarcastic but not spiteful.

Richard's mother, the Duchess of York, on the other hand, has learned to curse her own son. 'Thou cam'st on earth to make the earth my hell!' (IV.4.167). Her last words to Richard in the play are curses: 'Bloody thou art. Bloody will be thy end! / Shame serves thy life and doth thy death attend' (IV.4.195–6).

CHECKPOINT 19

In what other ways in Act I Scene 2 does Anne show what she thinks of Richard?

GLOSSARY
cacodemon evil spirit
want lack
infamy public wickedness, disgrace
bark ship
brook cope with, stand
Swills Drinks, slurps
wash hogwash, pigswill
trough place where pigs eat
embowelled disembowelled, cut open
Rude ragged Rough, uncomfortable
sullen dreary
unblown have not bloomed
sweets sweet-scented flowers
Avaunt Be gone!
diffused infection widespread plague
attend wait for

LANGUAGE OF PERSUASION

In *Richard III*, the use of words to persuade others is extremely important. There are three different areas where this can be seen: Richard with Anne and Queen Elizabeth; Richard and Buckingham working on other nobles or the Lord Mayor of London and citizens; and Richard and Richmond rallying their troops.

In return for Anne's insults, Richard offers sweet words and flattery. He 'renders good for bad, blessing for curses' (I.2.69). She calls him a devil. He calls her 'divine' (I.2.75). For her 'dungeon', he replies 'bed-chamber' (I.2.111); and for her 'mortal poison' when she spits at him, he says, 'Never came poison from so sweet a place' (I.2.146–7). In Act I Scene 3, Richard says he 'cannot flatter and look fair' (line 47), but we know already that he can, and better than most. Part of his game is to persuade others that he speaks honestly and is not a trickster himself!

CHECKPOINT 20

Richard is someone who would do well when interviewed on television. Think up some questions you would like him to be asked.

Richard's approach to Queen Elizabeth contains less flattery but shows the same ability to resist taunts. Elizabeth is outraged that he should want to marry her daughter: 'she cannot choose but hate thee' (IV.4.289). Richard, however, replies with a long list of reasons, including 'fair England's peace' (IV.4.343), why Princess Elizabeth should not hate him, but marry him. To every one of Queen Elizabeth's questions or objections, he has an answer.

Buckingham can use words as well as Richard. We see this particularly when he is talking to the Lord Mayor about the treachery of Hastings: 'I would have had you heard / The traitor speak,' he says (III.5.56–7). How unfortunate that the 'traitor' has already been killed and therefore cannot do so! Richard trusts Buckingham's ability to speak with the Lord Mayor and to spread lies about Edward IV and his children to the citizens. We see this again when Buckingham stage-manages and stars in the 'Make Richard king!' show in Act III Scene 7. In this scene both Buckingham and Richard use all their powers of persuasion to win over the citizens.

When it comes to the final part of the play, Richard tries to use words to encourage his supporters (see the summary of Act V

Scene 3). In his speech to his army Richard does his best to insult the enemy. He calls them 'vagabonds, rascals … base lackey peasants' (V.3.316–17) and their leader, Richmond, 'A milk-sop!' (V.3.325). He asks his supporters: 'Shall these enjoy our lands? – lie with our wives?' (V.3.336). Towards the end his words echo those of Richmond: 'Advance our standards! Set upon our foes!' (V.3.348), but his focus is more negative. Richard thinks of his enemies while Richmond draws on the courage of his men.

DIALOGUE

Much of the play is taken up with speeches rather than dialogue that feels like conversation. However, there are a number of places where the exchanges between characters are different. The conversation between Queen Elizabeth and her family at the beginning of Act I Scene 3 is one example. Another is the exchange between the two young princes and Richard in Act III Scene 1.

There is little comic dialogue except, of course, between the two murderers as they prepare to kill Clarence. When the second murderer says he is feeling guilty, the first murderer reminds him of the 'reward when the deed's done' (I.4.117). Immediately, the second murderer feels better: 'Zounds, he dies! I had forgot the reward' (I.4.118).

The conversation between the little Duke of York and his uncle Richard in Act III Scene 1 also could be seen as comic, but the undertones are even more deadly than those preceding Clarence's murder, so it is hard to laugh.

We can see another kind of dialogue in Act IV Scene 4 from line 343. Richard is trying to persuade Queen Elizabeth to help him win the hand of her daughter. Suddenly it becomes like a tennis match between two players, lines of dialogue whizzing back and forth between Richard and Elizabeth. There is a rhythm and repetition which is maintained until the pattern is broken by Elizabeth's longer speech and a series of half-lines (lines 368–77).

Overall, the closer characters are to each other – that is, the more comfortable they are in each other's company – the more

DID YOU KNOW?

In fact, it wasn't Richmond who led the troops into battle at Bosworth Field; it was his ally, the Earl of Oxford, who was the most experienced commander there.

GLOSSARY

lackey submissive, serving

standards flags

Zounds God's wounds (an exclamation, oath)

light hearted their dialogue will be. It is no surprise that in the ambitious world of *Richard III*, with its rivalry and plotting, such dialogue is rare.

LYRICAL DESCRIPTION

DID YOU KNOW?

Richard III was loved by **audiences** in Shakespeare's own lifetime, ranking in popularity with *Romeo and Juliet* and *Hamlet*. Six editions of the play were published between 1597 and 1622.

Shakespeare, as we know from his Sonnets and many plays, was a master of descriptive, lyrical language. We see little of this in *Richard III*. However, there is one section which is unlike the rest of the play, and that is the Duke of Clarence's speech describing his dream.

In Act I Scene 4, Clarence describes his dream to the keeper in the Tower of London. He paints a vivid picture of the underwater scene:

> Wedges of gold, great anchors, heaps of pearl,
> Inestimable stones, unvalued jewels –
> All scattered in the bottom of the sea!
> Some lay in dead men's skulls, and in the holes
> Where eyes did once inhabit … (I.4.26–30)

He also describes vividly a vision of hell where he is terrified by dreadful sights such as 'A shadow like an angel, with bright hair / Dabbled in blood' (I.4.53–4). So vivid are his words that the keeper himself is 'afraid … to hear you tell it' (I.4.65).

In *Richard III*, even the lyrical descriptions turn out to be nightmares!

THE TEXT IN PERFORMANCE

The performance of a play is very different from the play on the page. The script gives the actors the lines to speak, but Shakespeare gives very little guidance on how these lines should be spoken. Compare this with a modern play: it will probably have many instructions to the actors on how to present their lines, where and how to move – even what expressions to adopt. These instructions are called stage directions and there are relatively few of them in *Richard III*.

This being the case, the director and the actors have a lot of freedom. Think of the things that can affect the way we understand a particular line. Bear in mind that in filmed versions there are even more possibilities, including the use of close-up and camera angle.

- Tone of voice

- Expression

- Direction of gaze

- Actions before, during or after the line

- The reactions of other actors

- How the actor is lit

Take, for example, the simple line of Richard's – 'Nor none that live, I hope' – in reply to the young Prince of Wales, who has just said: 'I fear no uncles dead' (III.1.146–7). But the audience knows – or at least suspects – that the prince has every reason to be afraid of his uncle Richard. There are a number of points to consider here:

- Is Richard's tone jovial and upbeat or serious and grave – or is it perhaps spoken as a throwaway line, which dismisses its importance?

- What does Richard's expression convey? Concern? Love?

- Does Richard look directly at the prince? Or at Buckingham or the audience, perhaps knowingly …?

- What are Richard's actions before, during and after the line? Does he ruffle his nephew's hair – or does he give him the respect that the heir to the throne deserves?

- What are the reactions of other actors such as Buckingham and the young Duke of York? There are lots of other people around, including Lord Hastings, the Archbishop of Canterbury, the Lord Mayor of London and attendants. How do they react, if at all?

- Does the lighting pick out the speakers or light the whole stage?

And that is just one line! Consider how many decisions a director has to make in the course of an entire play.

CHECKPOINT 21

Pick some individual lines from different scenes of the play and see how many ways you can think of to present and perform each one.

CHECKPOINT 22

Where and how would you like to set the play? Could it be done in, say, a science fiction or a gangster setting?

Where actors stand and how they are arranged in relation to one another on the stage can also be important. Sometimes physical closeness suggests friendship. In some of the early scenes, for example, we might expect to see Queen Elizabeth's relations grouped together, with Lord Hastings and the Duke of Buckingham separate. How characters move is another consideration. Some will stand still while speaking; others will move about the stage. The way Richard moves with his 'deformities' will be particularly crucial.

Decisions about costume and the stage set will also influence the way we see the play. Directors often place the play in a modern or at least a twentieth-century setting. What are the advantages and disadvantages of this? (The reference to swords is one example of a difficulty.)

STRUCTURE

The structure of *Richard III* is very straightforward. Unlike many of Shakespeare's plays, there are no subplots to confuse or, equally, interest us. There are also few surprises along the way. We are kept informed, either directly or indirectly, by Richard as each new move is plotted.

The play, it seems, builds in a series of steps. At each step Richard is a little higher up the ladder and someone else has fallen off. It is with the murder of the princes that we begin to see power slipping away from Richard. The Earl of Richmond and the Marquis of Dorset have already gone, and Richard, through his own bad temper, has lost his most loyal and useful ally, Buckingham. The rest of the play is a story of further loss and confusion. Even Richard's conversation with Queen Elizabeth, where he seems on the way to achieving another of his goals, ends (we discover later) in failure.

Finally, in Act V, we see the ladder tottering. It takes only a sharp blow from Richmond to send it crashing.

Although the overall shape of the play is straightforward, there are rises and falls in the dramatic tension as the action proceeds:

- In Act I we move through three scenes, with more talk than action, to the tragicomedy of the Duke of Clarence's murder.

- In Act II there are several smaller shocks: the revelation of Clarence's death and, a scene later, of Edward's death; the unspoken threat to the princes; and the news of the arrest of Earl Rivers and Lord Grey.

- In Act III the tension builds with the sending of the princes to the Tower of London and Derby's warning to Hastings. This is followed rapidly by the execution of Rivers and Grey, and the arrest and killing of Lord Hastings. The rest of the act reduces the tension as Richard and Buckingham plot to have Richard crowned king.

- In Act IV the action builds to the quarrel between Buckingham and Richard and the murder of the princes. Throughout the rest of this act we learn of growing threats to Richard.

- In Act V everything builds towards the battle. The appearance of the ghosts and the rallying speeches to the troops are key elements in raising the tension. The pace is quick as the action shifts back and forth between the camps of Richard and Richmond. The climax comes, fittingly, in the last scene, and the audience is left on a high.

Directors of the play usually make cuts and alterations. The 1995 film version starring Ian McKellen made huge changes, for example. It is also the case that acting companies rarely have enough actors to play all the forty-odd characters in the original play. Frequently whole parts are cut, and sometimes characters are 'joined together', especially minor ones. Sometimes even major characters are removed; in one production at least, Margaret was left out.

Finally, although a battle is a good, clear way to finish a play, are there any loose ends at the close of *Richard III*? Do we know what happens to Queen Margaret, the Duchess of York and Queen Elizabeth? What will happen to Sir William Catesby and Sir James Tyrrel?

CHECKPOINT 23

Certain scenes in *Richard III* are repeated, with subtle differences, in the play. Can you think of any particular scenes which are mirrored or echoed later on?

EXAMINER'S SECRET

You could draw a timeline and add different colours for different characters, showing their rising or falling fortunes. Many will end with a sharp fall!

CHECKPOINT 24

Think about staging the play with a small cast. Which parts could you cut without losing too much that is important?

PART FOUR

THE TEST

UNDERSTANDING THE QUESTION

There are **four** different types of question that the examiner can ask you about *Richard III.* There are questions about:

1) Character and motivation: This means the examiner will ask you about a particular character. You will need to explain the reason the character is behaving in the way he or she is. You will be expected to look at the clues that Shakespeare gives and understand how the character's behaviour may be viewed by different characters. You will also be expected to understand how the character's behaviour may change over time. It is likely that you will be asked about the main characters of Richard, Buckingham, Queen Elizabeth or Anne, but the examiner may also ask you about Queen Margaret, the Duchess of York, Edward IV, Clarence or even Lord Hastings and the Earl of Derby.

2) Ideas, themes and issues: This means the examiner will ask you about one of the things that Shakespeare seems to be talking about in his play. You will be expected to understand what Shakespeare has to say about this idea, theme or issue, and you will need to provide **evidence** from the play to back up what you say. Themes such as lies and self-deceptions, and conscience are likely to be popular in questions, but the examiner may also ask you about other themes or ideas, such as the position of women or what we find out about fortune and its ups and downs.

3) The language of the text: This means the examiner will ask you about Shakespeare's choice of language, and the techniques he uses. You will be expected to pick out important examples and then talk about the effect these are meant to have on the audience. Therefore, with *Richard III,* you could be asked to discuss Shakespeare's use of curses and insults; how Richard persuades others; the way words are used to say one thing and mean another; or how language is used to gain the support of citizens or troops.

EXAMINER'S SECRET

Are there any moments in the play when you were taken by surprise? Don't be afraid to give a personal point of view as long as you can give a reason and it is relevant to your answer.

4) The text in performance: This means the examiner will ask you about the kind of decisions that you would make if you were directing a performance of the play. You need to think about what sort of impact these decisions would have on the audience. You could describe an actor using a certain type of facial expression or tone of voice. You will need to base your ideas about a character's appearance or the mood of a scene on what you find in the play itself. With *Richard III* you could be asked to direct a certain character through part of a scene. For example, you could direct an actor playing Richard through two extracts, explaining how the actor should show his reactions, and giving reasons for your suggestions.

In class, you will have been preparing two or three sections of the play. In the exam, the examiner will have chosen two short extracts from these sections for you to write about.

This means that as long as you can understand the question you will know exactly what the examiner is expecting to see in the answer that you give. For instance:

Act II Scene 2 lines 112–54

Act IV Scene 2 lines 1–45

How do these two extracts show the changing relationship between Buckingham and Richard?

What are the **key words** in this question? The names **Buckingham** and **Richard** tell us whom we are to focus on but also make it clear to us that we are answering a **character and motivation** question. This means we need to look not just at the characters of Richard and Buckingham, but at the way they affect each other. This is more focused and precise than being asked to write about their characters in a general way. Here the examiner has given some extra help by using the word **change**. We are clearly expected to show that what we see happening between Richard and Buckingham in the second extract is a contrast to what we see in the first extract. The word **show** is also important – a reminder that we must use **evidence** from the extracts to back up what we say. It is important that we look only at the two extracts

EXAMINER'S SECRET

Whenever you are thinking about the play, it is helpful to put the book out of your mind and try to see the actions taking place in 3D on a stage. This is particularly useful when answering questions about the **text** in performance.

DID YOU KNOW?

Although it wasn't published until 1597, *Richard III* was probably written around 1593 and was one of Shakespeare's earliest plays.

chosen by the examiner. When it comes to your test, the extracts will be provided in the test booklet. This means that you can read these over before you begin to plan your answer.

LOOKING AT THE EVIDENCE

It is very important to make sure your answer is closely linked to what happens in the extracts you have been given. Let's imagine we are still trying to answer the question about Richard and Buckingham. When discussing Richard and Buckingham it would be easy to talk about some different aspects of their characters, such as Richard's sly wooing of Anne or Buckingham's regret when he dies. However, these things do not take place in the scenes the examiner has asked us to write about and they do not directly concern the **relationship** between the two men. We need to look at these extracts and see what evidence we can find to help us talk about Richard and Buckingham and how they relate with each other.

What evidence do we have?

Act II Scene 2 lines 112–54

- Buckingham gives advice to the other nobles and sets out a plan.

- Richard agrees, and after the others have left Buckingham explains more of his plan.

- Richard praises Buckingham.

Act IV Scene 2 lines 1–45

- Richard has formed a plan and wants Buckingham's support.

- Buckingham asks for more time.

- Richard is angry, and finds someone else to carry out his wishes.

- Richard will no longer confide in Buckingham.

Once we have found the evidence from the extracts we can see that the relationship between Richard and Buckingham is close at first. They are conspirators. We can see in the first extract that Buckingham is taking the lead and that Richard is grateful to him. In the second extract we see the opposite, however. Richard is driving the action and Buckingham is hanging back, earning not gratitude but dislike. Although they are still plotting together, their relationship has changed.

By looking at the evidence, we have found an answer to our question. We have also made sure that this evidence is from the correct part of the play.

DID YOU KNOW?
The word *conspire* comes from Latin words which mean 'to breathe together'. This means it makes sense to have two conspiring actors standing very close to each other on stage.

WRITING YOUR ANSWER

The examiner is asking you to write about two extracts from the set scenes. You are asked to do this because the examiner wants to see if you can follow **developments** between the scenes, comment on contrasts and **comparisons**, or consider the same issues at different moments. Looking at different sections should also encourage you to come up with a **variety** of ideas. A good way to approach these questions is to look at each scene, one at a time. However, you must make connections between the scenes, using connectives to help you.

It is important that you **structure** your answer well. This means thinking about what you will write at the start, the middle and the end of your essay. Although you won't have much time to plan your answer in the test, as soon as you read a question you should begin thinking about how best to tackle it. A good structure will help you make your points clearly and allow your **argument** to flow.

A POSSIBLE STRUCTURE

The answer to the question about Richard and Buckingham may look something like this:

1) Introduction
Introduce Richard and Buckingham. *Briefly* say how they behave towards each other in the two extracts.

2) Section 1: Act II Scene 2 lines 112–54

- We see Buckingham making arrangements for bringing the Prince of Wales to London and explaining why he should be 'fetched' with 'some little train' (II.2.120–1). He is taking the lead and Richard follows.

- The two speak in confidence after the others have left. They seem to be talking as equals.

- As they leave, Richard tells Buckingham he is 'My other self' (II.2.151). We have no reason to believe he does not mean it.

3) Section 2: Act IV Scene 2 lines 1–45

- Richard is now king and takes the lead. He questions Buckingham as a teacher might question a pupil. He is testing him.

- Richard wants the princes dead, but Buckingham is unsure. Buckingham hesitates and this makes Richard very angry.

- Richard decides that their relationship as conspirators is over. They are definitely no longer equals.

4) Conclusion

Answer the question: What changes have taken place? How is the relationship different in the two extracts?

This answer is split into four sections. The aims of an introduction and a conclusion are the same no matter what the question. The introduction aims to say something about the **key words** in the question. It also aims to say briefly how both the extracts are linked to those key words. The conclusion always aims to answer the question in brief. The middle two sections look at the extracts closely. Notice how the bullet points directly answer the question. It is important that each bullet point becomes one paragraph in your essay, i.e. with this structure you would write at least six short paragraphs, plus an introduction and conclusion.

DID YOU KNOW?
Richard III was first published in 1597 as a **tragedy**. In 1623 it appeared in the First Folio (the first collected edition of Shakespeare's plays) in the history section.

ADDING DETAIL TO YOUR STRUCTURE

Of course, your basic structure is not the essay itself. You need to add three important things when writing your answer:

1. Quotations which are relevant to the points you want to make

2. Detailed explanations of your points

3. Links between the two extracts

For example, a suitable quotation is needed for the following point:

- Richard wants the princes dead, but Buckingham is unsure. Buckingham hesitates and this makes Richard very angry.

The quotation could be:

> Thy kindness freezes.
> Say, have I thy consent that they shall die?

The detailed explanation could be:

> **Buckingham has not taken the hint that Richard wants Prince Edward and his brother dead. Perhaps he does realise what Richard means but does not want to admit it. Richard's anger begins to show through. He is annoyed and accuses Buckingham of being cold towards him. The use of the word 'freezes' underlines the cooling of their friendship. Richard finally demands an answer from Buckingham. He asks for Buckingham's 'consent' but it is clear it is only his support he needs, as Richard now has all the power.**

The link to the first extract could be:

> **This is very different from Buckingham's eagerness to be part of Richard's bid for power in Act II. The audience is made to wonder what Buckingham's hesitation might mean.**

This can be done for **every** bullet point in your structure. In other words, for each paragraph you need to:

- make your point

- add supporting quotation(s)

GLOSSARY

little train small troop of attendants

EXAMINER'S SECRET

Short references to other parts of *Richard III* show that you know the whole play, not just the set scenes – but keep these very brief.

- add some detailed explanation

- add a link to the other extracts (and sometimes links to elsewhere in the play)

PLANNING IN THE TEST ITSELF

Of course, in the actual test, you will not be able to write out the full structure as we have done above. You will need to reduce your structure to a **basic plan** as follows:

Introduction

- The part played by Buckingham and Richard in the play.

- How their relationship appears in the two extracts.

Extract 1

- Buckingham takes the lead in organising the Prince of Wales's return.

- He and Richard plot together.

- Richard treats him as a friend and equal.

Extract 2

- Richard tests the level of Buckingham's support.

- Buckingham wants time to think and Richard is angry.

- Richard will no longer treat Buckingham as a friend and an equal.

Conclusion

Richard and Buckingham start as close friends but this changes when Buckingham won't support the princes' murder. Friends become enemies.

In addition, you may want to note down quickly a few key words from the extracts, which you plan to use to support your ideas.

EXAMINER'S SECRET

Plan your answer, then you won't repeat yourself. And stick to your plan: students who don't often run out of time.

HOW TO USE QUOTATIONS

CHOOSING THE RIGHT QUOTATION

As you read through the test booklet you might have made notes, on a separate sheet, of words from the play that look useful for your essay. In writing your essay, you need to find a way of inserting these words, called quotations, into your writing. In order to choose good quotations you first need to know how to use them.

Quotations can be used in different ways:

- to prove what you are saying is true

- to enable you to make an interesting and detailed point about a character, theme, etc.

You can use both these types of quotations in your essay. However, finding quotations that prove what you are saying is true *and* allow you to make interesting and original points will get you the highest level in the test. Therefore, when you are choosing a quotation you need to ask yourself (a) does it prove my point and (b) what can I say about it?

HOW TO PUT THE QUOTATIONS IN YOUR ESSAY

The examiner asks you to **select** and **retrieve** information from the play. You are also expected to be able to use quotations successfully, including them at the right points in your essay. There are two ways of doing this:

1. You can stop your paragraph and then write out the short part of the play that you have selected.

2. You can take Shakespeare's words and make them flow into your sentence. This is called **embedding** the quotation.

Method 1: Separated quotations

When you want to discuss a quotation in detail you may want to make your point, drop down a line, and then write in your quotation. This method of using quotations is shown below:

EXAMINER'S SECRET

Be prepared to see and describe characters in your own way. It is easy to describe Richard as evil, but more interesting to say 'Richard is evil, but ...' Remember that 'but' and 'however' can be useful words.

We can see that Richard is angry from the way he bites his lip. It seems that he has been wondering if Buckingham will give him complete support because he says:

> now do I play the touch,
> To try if thou be current gold indeed.

Because the murder of the princes is a step further than they have taken so far, Richard needs to see if Buckingham is with him or not. Perhaps he suspects from Buckingham's manner that he can no longer trust him. Shakespeare uses the metaphor of testing gold to see if it is 'current' or genuine to show how Richard plans to test or 'try' Buckingham. Comparing Buckingham to 'gold' suggests that Richard puts a high price on Buckingham's support.

Notice how this method clearly separates the quotation so that you can comment on Shakespeare's language, and what it says about the characters and their attitudes. By moving down a line you are making it clear to the examiner that this is a quotation you are going to say something important about.

Method 2: Embedding

Sometimes, however, you may want to use quotations from the play as a way of illustrating your points clearly without breaking the flow of your paragraph. Inserting, or embedding, small quotations into your sentences will show the examiner that you are taking your ideas directly from the play. Notice how this is done below:

Later in Act IV Scene 2, we see how Richard has decided to carry on without Buckingham. He no longer wants Buckingham to be 'neighbour to my counsels' because he is too 'considerate' and too 'circumspect'. Richard does not want anything except unquestioning obedience. He will now rely on 'iron-witted fools' who will act without asking questions. Later in the same scene Buckingham returns but Richard will not listen to him. Buckingham is wise enough to know what this means. Not only are Richard and he no longer equals, they are not even leader and trusted ally. There is no middle way. Having failed Richard, Buckingham will be seen as a potential enemy. The relationship is over.

This answer is excellent because intelligent points are made using short quotations. Using quotations in this way has the advantage of showing the examiner that you can retrieve information from the text while at the same time allowing your essay to flow.

IMPROVE YOUR LEVEL

In the Key Stage 3 Reading test, there are four possible grades, or levels, that you can achieve: Levels 4–7. It is important that you know what it is that the questions expect from you, and how you can achieve the level you deserve.

A GENERAL GUIDE

Level 5 will be given when:

- You have focused clearly on the question.

- You show a generally clear understanding of the main points.

- You have used well-chosen evidence or quotations.

- You have developed some of your arguments.

- Your general writing is clear, if not always as **fluent** as it could be.

Higher levels will be given when:

- You have focused on the question clearly throughout.

- Your evidence and quotations are entirely suitable.

- You have suggested alternative, or original, ideas.

- You have shown **insight** (looked beyond the obvious).

- Your general writing is fluent and **coherent** (reads very well).

So, what would this actually mean if you were answering a question on *Richard III*?

GLOSSARY

play the touch act the touchstone (a stone used for testing the quality of gold)

considerate thoughtful, careful

circumspect cautious, thoughtful

iron-witted stupid

1) Character and motivation

Character questions are likely to ask you about the impression you get of a character because of the way they behave or the things they say. For instance, the examiner may ask you about the impression you get of Richard in Act I Scene 2 lines 115–230 and in Act III Scene 4 lines 1–78. You might point out that Richard is very persuasive in the first extract, and then mention that his comment after Anne has left shows the lack of respect he has for her: 'Was ever woman in this humour wooed?' (I.2.228). In the second extract we see other qualities completely: ruthlessness and anger. A Level 5 answer would conclude that Richard is a person of many different faces, public and private.

CHECKPOINT 25

When Richard claims that his withered arm is a result of being bewitched, can he expect anyone to believe him?

- A higher level answer would add less obvious examples. For instance, Lord Hastings's loyalty to the recently dead King Edward IV and his heirs is mocked by Richard as he reports his findings to Buckingham: 'His master's child – as worshipfully he terms it' (III.4.39). Richard has no time for loyalty to anyone but himself.

- A higher level answer would offer an alternative view suggesting that we can never believe what Richard is telling us, even when he appears to criticise himself. He can play on his 'deformity' when he chooses, pretend to be religious or even exaggerate his anger. Sometimes we get the impression that he does not care if others see through him.

2) Ideas, themes and issues

Ideas, themes and issues questions will ask you to talk about one of the things that Shakespeare has been concerned about in the play. You will be expected to explore the evidence and the different ways of looking at this evidence. For instance, the examiner may ask you how the theme of conscience is dealt with in Act V Scene 1 and Act V Scene 3 lines 118–222. You might describe how Buckingham accepts that his wrong doing is now being punished. He sees the justice in Margaret's curse coming true and goes to his execution calmly. A Level 5 answer would say that Buckingham's conscience prompts him to curse Richard and pray for Richmond's success.

- A higher level answer would **explore** the way the **language** of Buckingham contrasts with that of Richard and how this reflects their consciences.

- A higher level answer would write about this idea **fluently**.

3) The language of the text

Language questions will ask you to look at the way that Shakespeare uses language in two extracts and the effect this has on the audience. For instance, you may be asked to talk about the way characters use language prior to their death, referring to Act III Scene 3 and Act V Scene 1. A Level 5 answer would mention the way Earl Rivers, Lord Grey and Sir Thomas Vaughan, and then Buckingham talk about justice, blame and Queen Margaret's curses, which they recall with almost the same words.

- A higher level answer would **develop** this idea, looking at the differences in the words used by Rivers, Grey and Vaughan compared with those used by the Duke of Buckingham.

- A higher level answer would also **explore** in more **subtle detail** the nature of these speeches. Buckingham's is a calm meditation to himself. Rivers, Grey and Vaughan address a number of audiences – Ratcliffe, God and each other – and their words are full of exclamations and curses of their own.

4) The text in performance

Performance questions will ask you to think like a director and consider how the play should be performed. They will ask you to focus on two extracts and explore how they might be performed differently. For instance, they may ask you to look at the performance of Richard in Act I Scene 3 lines 42–132 and compare it with his performance in Act IV Scene 4 lines 432–538. A Level 5 answer would point out how Richard controls events in the earlier act. An actor could portray him as being completely in control, and even enjoying himself. In the later scene he contradicts himself, has no clear plan and even strikes a messenger for bringing bad news. A higher level answer would need to be much more **developed**:

EXAMINER'S SECRET
You can include some personal views in your essays, as long as you keep them brief. For example, you could express some sympathy for Buckingham, despite his misdeeds.

EXAMINER'S SECRET

As you are writing, keep asking yourself: 'Am I answering the question I've been set?'

- It would show **insight** into Richard's world. It might mention how he cannot control Margaret in the first extract and suggest that some of his anger might be real. It would also go on to say that towards the end of the second extract, Richard regains control and becomes the soldier again.

- A higher level answer would also explore the function of these extracts. The first establishes Richard's mastery of events, while the later scene shows the decline in Richard's control and also provides useful information to the audience about the growing opposition to him.

FURTHER QUESTIONS

Here are eight sample test questions you can use for practice. Try answering each one using the advice provided in these Notes. You could spend 5 minutes writing a short plan before you start each essay, to get in practice for the test.

1 *Act I Scene 2 lines 115–230*

Act III Scene 4 lines 22–78

What impression do you get of Richard's character in these extracts?

2 *Act I Scene 1 lines 1–69*

Act IV Scene 2 lines 1–75

What are the motives that drive Richard in these extracts?

3 *Act V Scene 1 (complete scene)*

Act V Scene 3 lines 118–206

What do these two extracts say about conscience?

4 *Act II Scene 4 lines 1–66*

Act IV Scene 1 lines 28–end of the scene

What is the role of the women in these extracts?

5 *Act I Scene 4 lines 1–74*

Act V Scene 3 lines 177–222

Compare the language of dreams used by the Duke of Clarence and by Richard in these extracts.

6 *Act III Scene 3 (complete scene)*

Act V Scene 1 (complete scene)

How do characters use language to discuss their deaths in these extracts?

7 *Act I Scene 2 lines 91–225*

Act IV Scene 4 lines 270–345

Explain how the actor playing Richard should show his power in these extracts and give reasons for your suggestions.

9 *Act I Scene 2 lines 93–225*

Act IV Scene 1 lines 28–96

How could a director help to show Anne's mood in these extracts?

aside   words spoken in a play that are meant to be heard by the audience but not by all the characters on stage

audience   people watching a play

blank verse   unrhymed lines of poetry, usually written in iambic pentameter

character(s)   either a person in a play, novel, etc., or his or her personality

comedy   a type of literature that is humorous and usually light-hearted

connectives   words or phrases that link ideas or sentences, such as 'however', 'in the same way', etc.

contrast   difference

costume   items of clothing worn by the actors

dialogue   conversation between characters

director   the person responsible for the way a play is acted and interpreted

(dramatic) irony   when the audience knows more than the characters on the stage

(dramatic) tension   techniques used to build anticipation or suspense in the audience

extended metaphor   a comparison which uses the same idea more than once

function   the part something or someone plays in a drama

iambic pentameter   a ten-syllable line of poetry, where every second beat of the rhythm is emphasised

image (imagery)   an image is a picture created in the mind by the use of language. The picture gives more meaning to an idea. Imagery is the use of these pictures in a piece of writing

impact   the powerful effect that a word, phrase

or event has on the characters and audience

interpret   to find your own meaning in a text

irony   when you expect the opposite to be true; or something very unlikely takes place which is the last thing you would expect to happen

lyrical   a musical, flowing type of language, usually poetry

main plot   the most important storyline in the play

metaphor   a direct comparison

pathos   feelings of sympathy or pity towards a character

performance   the play as it is acted, rather than as a written text

personification   describing a thing as though it is a person and has feelings

phrases   groups of words which don't make a full sentence

poetry   a type of writing that usually uses rhythm and rhyme, and is set out in lines rather than sentences

production   the business of putting on a play, including the performance

prop   any object used on stage by the actors in a play, e.g. a book, a sword or a candle

prose   ordinary speech or writing, not poetry

pun   a play on words (see word play), which finds different meanings for the same word

quotation   exact words or phrases taken from the play and used in an essay to make a point

revelation   the moment when something important is revealed to the audience

rhyme   the use of words which have the same or similar sounds in one or more lines of verse rhythm   the 'beat' or patterns of sound in speech

role   part in a play

scene   a part of an act in a play

scenery   the backdrop and other furniture that make up the set on a stage

simile   a suggested comparison using 'like' or 'as'

soliloquy   a speech made by a character where he or she seems to be talking to themselves. This is usually used to reveal the character's thoughts to the audience

sound effects   a sound which creates an effect on stage, e.g. thunder or explosions

special effects   visual effects usually used in film and television productions, such as making people disappear or changing their appearance over time

stage direction   the part of the script, provided by the writer, that suggests how the characters should move, speak etc.

staging   putting on a play

subplot   a storyline which is less important than the main plot

suspense   a feeling that something is about to happen

symbol   something that is meant to represent an idea, e.g. a heart is a symbol of love

text   the play as it is written on paper

themes   the messages or ideas within a play

tragedy   a play that usually has an unhappy or cruel ending, and contains dark messages about life

tragicomedy   a type of play that combines tragedy and comedy so that serious events are made more light hearted, but also more ironic

verse   lines written with a specific length and set to a rhythm, like poetry

word play   clever use of words to make jokes and witty comments, i.e. puns

CHECKPOINT 1

- He seems to be taking you into his confidence.
- You are more likely to believe what he says.
- You are drawn closer to him, like it or not.

CHECKPOINT 2

- The actor playing Richard might use expressions and gestures to make this scene believable. The tone of his voice, together with pauses in his speech, might also be used to suggest real affection and sorrow.
- The actor playing Anne might try to show that she is torn between revulsion and fascination.
- Anne has no one else to protect her now.
- Perhaps she would like to retain some of the advantages of her status.

CHECKPOINT 3

- Her presence is a continuing reminder to the audience – and the other characters – of the past: the Wars of the Roses and all the bloodshed and violence.
- In her role as 'prophetess' she predicts the fate of many, and acts as a commentator on the events unfolding around her.
- At the start of the play, Margaret is the only one who sees through Richard's public disguise to the real face beneath. She gives us and the other characters a different viewpoint on the Duke of Gloucester.
- Eventually she becomes a kind of inspiration to the other women, teaching them how to curse their enemies.

CHECKPOINT 4

- Margaret curses seven people directly by name: Edward IV, Queen Elizabeth, Richard, Lord Hastings, Earl Rivers, the Marquis of Dorset and the Prince of Wales.

- She also curses the rest of Queen Elizabeth's children (the Duke of York, Princess Elizabeth and Lord Grey) when she proclaims: 'Long may'st thou live to wail thy children's death' (I.3.203) and 'Die neither mother, wife' (I.3.208).
- She does not so much curse Buckingham as warn him.

CHECKPOINT 5

- The two murderers are two low characters who have come to kill a man, and are not of noble birth like most of the other characters. It is perhaps fitting, therefore, that they should talk in ordinary prose, not poetry.
- It makes their conversation seem more informal, and suggests the second murderer's uncertainty and changes of mind.
- It is significant that they do not speak in prose the whole time. Later, when Clarence tries to persuade them not to kill him, they reply to him in blank verse. It is as if his emotional and moving speech in verse has rubbed off on them.

CHECKPOINT 6

- They will use Sir William Catesby to spy on Hastings.
- Hastings trusts Catesby and so he is unlikely to suspect what is really going on.

CHECKPOINT 7

- Margaret cursed them in Act I Scene 3.
- They were responsible for the death of her husband and son – and the loss of her queenly status.

CHECKPOINT 8

- Richard accuses Hastings of protecting those who have 'bewitched' him.

- He hasn't been bewitched, so the accusation is clearly false.
- On the other hand, Hastings's lover, Mistress Shore, is a close friend of Queen Elizabeth's, who does not like or trust Richard. Richard may believe all these people are plotting against him in some way.

CHECKPOINT 9

- Buckingham implies that Richard is religious and Edward IV was not.
- He states that Richard is pure and honourable and that Edward IV was lecherous.
- He says that Edward IV's sons are not lawful and therefore not proper heirs to the crown of England.

CHECKPOINT 10

- We don't know why Brakenbury says this. It is one of Shakespeare's mysterious lines which make us wonder.
- It is quite likely, though, that Brakenbury has some 'inside' knowledge.

CHECKPOINT 11

- The actor playing Buckingham could be cold here, or pretend to be friendly. Either of these would work and be true to the play.
- He could also portray Buckingham as being hesitant: he is losing his influence with Richard and knows it.
- Buckingham might also act in a deadpan manner so that no one can tell what he is thinking. You may think of others.

CHECKPOINT 12

- Margaret compares Richard to a dog, a hog, a toad and a spider.

CHECKPOINT 13

- Richard argues that the marriage will secure the well-being of Elizabeth's children and grandchildren.
- He tells her he loves her daughter.
- He says he cannot undo what has been done, but her daughter being queen will be some compensation for the dead princes.
- He argues that the marriage will bring peace to the country.
- Elizabeth might agree because she believes Richard – or at least half believes him and wants a quiet life.
- She might be afraid of what he will do if she gives a definite no.

CHECKPOINT 14

- It is likely that most people are on Richmond's side.
- Even if they are not totally on Richmond's side, they are not going to support Richard in large numbers.

CHECKPOINT 15

- Both Richmond and Richard call on St George, the patron saint of England.
- His name is easy to use because it is familiar to the people and encourages them to be patriotic.

CHECKPOINT 16

- This really is a matter of opinion. Richard probably reveals too much of his thoughts in his asides and soliloquies for the audience to be fooled by his acting and pretence.
- The audience may be *surprised* by what he does, which is a slightly different thing.

CHECKPOINT 17

- It is hard to see any.

- However, Margaret's curses have an effect on the way other characters feel.
- And the women do, of course, influence the feelings of the audience.

CHECKPOINT 18
- There are many examples of modern-day celebrities who are both praised and criticised in the papers, from pop stars to actors, footballers to supermodels.
- In fairy tales the wicked queen in *Snow White* and the ugly sisters in *Cinderella* are similar to Richard: they treat other people badly but are punished themselves in the end.

CHECKPOINT 19
- She spits at Richard.
- She also takes his sword, which Richard offers, and moves as if she is about to stab him.

CHECKPOINT 20
- 'Did you think murdering children was a good way to advance your career, Mr York?'
- 'Just what did happen to your wife?'
- 'Do you have any friends?'
- You will be able to think of others – and maybe some answers!

CHECKPOINT 21
- Images of wrecks and skulls and jewels, perhaps shown through a green filter, could be projected onto a screen or onto the whole stage area during Clarence's lines beginning 'Methoughts I saw a thousand fearful wrecks' (I.4.24–33).
- The ghosts appearing to Richmond and Richard in Act V Scene 3 could use voice-overs. The lighting could change from white to red according to whether they are speaking to Richmond or to Richard.

CHECKPOINT 22
- An idea for a gangster setting would be to have certain parts of the action set in a bar.
- In Act I Scene 2, for example, two men in heavy coats bring in Henry VI's body and lay it across some chairs. Anne, dressed as a gangster's wife, follows and falls to her knees beside the body, weeping.
- Richard watches from the doorway to the cellar, collar turned up and hat pulled down.
- Anne speaks her lines. As the men go to pick up the body, Richard speaks his line sharply from the semi-darkness: 'Stay, you that bear the corpse, and set it down' (I.2.33).

CHECKPOINT 23
- Richard's wooing of Lady Anne is mirrored later on in his wooing of Elizabeth.
- Clarence has 'fearful dreams' shortly before he is killed (I.4.3). Later Richard is visited by ghosts in a 'fearful dream' (V.3.212).
- Lord Hastings, an adviser to the king, is arrested and executed. Later, another of the king's advisers is arrested and executed: this time the Duke of Buckingham.

CHECKPOINT 24
- This is obviously a matter of judgement, but many of the courtiers could be combined.
- The Marquis of Dorset is often omitted, as is the Bishop of Ely.

CHECKPOINT 25
- Probably not. After all, it was a deformity at birth and can hardly have been brought about recently by his enemies!
- But no one dares to contradict him.

TEST YOURSELF
ACT I

1. Richard

2. Lady Anne

3. Queen Elizabeth

4. Queen Margaret

5. Duke of Clarence

6. He blames his 'deformity': he is not of a 'fair proportion' like other men.

7. King Edward IV has heard a prophecy that someone whose name begins with G will kill his heirs. The Duke of Clarence is called George.

8. Clarence is the elder brother and would have a better claim to the throne than his younger brother Richard.

9. Lady Anne is the widow of the previous king's son. If Richard marries her, he takes care of one possible source of opposition.

10. Margaret was the wife of the previous, deposed king, Henry VI.

ACT II

1. King Edward IV

2. Duchess of York

3. Duke of Buckingham

4. Citizen 3

5. Queen Elizabeth

6. Apart from King Edward's desire to establish peace in the country he has recently taken over, he fears he does not have long to live and wishes to see old quarrels resolved.

7. Edward IV had sent a message to pardon the Duke of Clarence.

8. Buckingham claims that too large a body of soldiers and nobles might alarm people, given the wars that have just ended. In fact, he is anxious to make sure that the Prince of Wales doesn't fall into anyone else's hands.

9. They are sent to Pomfret Castle.

10. Queen Elizabeth takes her son to seek the sanctuary (safety) of the Church.

ACT III

1. Richard

2. Edward, Prince of Wales

3. Duke of Buckingham

4. Richard

5. Richard

6. The young Duke of York is still with his mother, Queen Elizabeth, in the sanctuary of the Church.

7. He warns Hastings that Richard may have him imprisoned or killed.

8. He accuses Elizabeth of bewitching him and causing his bodily deformities.

9. 'God save Richard, England's royal king!'

10. Two bishops are the props; Richard is the Christian prince.

ACT IV

1. Queen Elizabeth

2. Queen Elizabeth

3. Sir James Tyrrel

4. Richard

5. Earl of Derby

6. She asks Margaret for help to curse Richard.

7. Buckingham will not give Richard his immediate support for the murder of the princes.

8. Richard will not give Buckingham the reward he was promised. Buckingham is now afraid for his life.

9. He says that he loves Elizabeth's daughter. He promises Elizabeth that marriage to her daughter will make up for the wrongs done to her relations, and will bring about peace.

10. Richard is holding Derby's son hostage.

ACT V

1. Duke of Buckingham

2. Earl of Richmond

3. Ghost of Henry VI

4. Ghost of Buckingham

5. Earl of Richmond

6. He says that Richard's supporters only back him because they are afraid.

7. Eleven ghosts appear to Richard and Richmond.

8. The ghosts terrify Richard and make him doubt the outcome of the battle. They also bring home the extent of his misdeeds.

9. To kill Richmond.

10. By marrying the young Princess Elizabeth, Edward IV's daughter.

GCSE

Maya Angelou
I Know Why the Caged Bird Sings

Jane Austen
Pride and Prejudice

Alan Ayckbourn
Absent Friends

Elizabeth Barrett Browning
Selected Poems

Robert Bolt
A Man for All Seasons

Harold Brighouse
Hobson's Choice

Charlotte Brontë
Jane Eyre

Emily Brontë
Wuthering Heights

Brian Clark
Whose Life is it Anyway?

Robert Cormier
Heroes

Shelagh Delaney
A Taste of Honey

Charles Dickens
David Copperfield
Great Expectations
Hard Times
Oliver Twist
Selected Stories

Roddy Doyle
Paddy Clarke Ha Ha Ha

George Eliot
Silas Marner
The Mill on the Floss

Anne Frank
The Diary of a Young Girl

William Golding
Lord of the Flies

Oliver Goldsmith
She Stoops to Conquer

Willis Hall
The Long and the Short and the Tall

Thomas Hardy
Far from the Madding Crowd
The Mayor of Casterbridge
Tess of the d'Urbervilles
The Withered Arm and other Wessex Tales

L. P. Hartley
The Go-Between

Seamus Heaney
Selected Poems

Susan Hill
I'm the King of the Castle

Barry Hines
A Kestrel for a Knave

Louise Lawrence
Children of the Dust

Harper Lee
To Kill a Mockingbird

Laurie Lee
Cider with Rosie

Arthur Miller
The Crucible
A View from the Bridge

Robert O'Brien
Z for Zachariah

Frank O'Connor
My Oedipus Complex and Other Stories

George Orwell
Animal Farm

J. B. Priestley
An Inspector Calls
When We Are Married

Willy Russell
Educating Rita
Our Day Out

J. D. Salinger
The Catcher in the Rye

William Shakespeare
Henry IV Part I
Henry V
Julius Caesar
Macbeth
The Merchant of Venice
A Midsummer Night's Dream
Much Ado About Nothing
Romeo and Juliet
The Tempest
Twelfth Night

George Bernard Shaw
Pygmalion

Mary Shelley
Frankenstein

R. C. Sherriff
Journey's End

Rukshana Smith
Salt on the Snow

John Steinbeck
Of Mice and Men

Robert Louis Stevenson
Dr Jekyll and Mr Hyde

Jonathan Swift
Gulliver's Travels

Robert Swindells
Daz 4 Zoe

Mildred D. Taylor
Roll of Thunder, Hear My Cry

Mark Twain
Huckleberry Finn

James Watson
Talking in Whispers

Edith Wharton
Ethan Frome

William Wordsworth
Selected Poems

A Choice of Poets

Mystery Stories of the Nineteenth Century including The Signalman

Nineteenth Century Short Stories

Poetry of the First World War

Six Women Poets

For the AQA Anthology:

Duffy and Armitage & Pre-1914 Poetry

Heaney and Clarke & Pre-1914 Poetry

Poems from Different Cultures

Key Stage 3

William Shakespeare
Henry V
Macbeth
Much Ado About Nothing
Richard III
The Tempest

Margaret Atwood
Cat's Eye
The Handmaid's Tale

Jane Austen
Emma
Mansfield Park
Persuasion
Pride and Prejudice
Sense and Sensibility

William Blake
Songs of Innocence and of Experience

Charlotte Brontë
Jane Eyre
Villette

Emily Brontë
Wuthering Heights

Angela Carter
Nights at the Circus
Wise Children

Geoffrey Chaucer
The Franklin's Prologue and Tale
The Merchant's Prologue and Tale
The Miller's Prologue and Tale
The Prologue to the Canterbury Tales
The Wife of Bath's Prologue and Tale

Samuel Coleridge
Selected Poems

Joseph Conrad
Heart of Darkness

Daniel Defoe
Moll Flanders

Charles Dickens
Bleak House
Great Expectations
Hard Times

Emily Dickinson
Selected Poems

John Donne
Selected Poems

Carol Ann Duffy
Selected Poems

George Eliot
Middlemarch
The Mill on the Floss

T. S. Eliot
Selected Poems
The Waste Land

F. Scott Fitzgerald
The Great Gatsby

E. M. Forster
A Passage to India

Charles Frazier
Cold Mountain

Brian Friel
Making History
Translations

William Golding
The Spire

Thomas Hardy
Jude the Obscure
The Mayor of Casterbridge
The Return of the Native
Selected Poems
Tess of the d'Urbervilles

Nathaniel Hawthorne
The Scarlet Letter

Seamus Heaney
Selected Poems from 'Opened Ground'

Homer
The Iliad
The Odyssey

Aldous Huxley
Brave New World

Kazuo Ishiguro
The Remains of the Day

Ben Jonson
The Alchemist

James Joyce
Dubliners

John Keats
Selected Poems

Philip Larkin
The Whitsun Weddings and Selected Poems

Christopher Marlowe
Doctor Faustus
Edward II

Ian McEwan
Atonement

Arthur Miller
Death of a Salesman

John Milton
Paradise Lost Books I & II

Toni Morrison
Beloved

George Orwell
Nineteen Eighty-Four

Sylvia Plath
Selected Poems

Alexander Pope
Rape of the Lock & Selected Poems

William Shakespeare
Antony and Cleopatra
As You Like It
Hamlet
Henry IV Part I
King Lear
Macbeth
Measure for Measure
The Merchant of Venice
A Midsummer Night's Dream
Much Ado About Nothing
Othello
Richard II
Richard III
Romeo and Juliet
The Taming of the Shrew
The Tempest
Twelfth Night
The Winter's Tale

George Bernard Shaw
Saint Joan

Mary Shelley
Frankenstein

Bram Stoker
Dracula

Jonathan Swift
Gulliver's Travels and A Modest Proposal

Alfred Tennyson
Selected Poems

Alice Walker
The Color Purple

John Webster
The Duchess of Malfi

Oscar Wilde
The Importance of Being Earnest

Tennessee Williams
A Streetcar Named Desire
The Glass Menagerie

Jeanette Winterson
Oranges Are Not the Only Fruit

Virginia Woolf
To the Lighthouse

William Wordsworth
The Prelude and Selected Poems

W. B. Yeats
Selected Poems

Metaphysical Poets